ZEBULON PIKE
Soldier and Explorer

ZEBULON PIKE

SOLDIER AND EXPLORER

BY LEONARD WIBBERLEY

FUNK & WAGNALLS COMPANY, NEW YORK

AUTHOR'S NOTE

Few soldiers in American history have been as consistently maligned as Zebulon Montgomery Pike, the man after whom Pike's Peak in Colorado is named. It was Pike's misfortune to serve under General James Wilkinson, a commanding officer of overwhelming ambition and dubious loyalty. Wilkinson was implicated in the great Wilkinson-Burr conspiracy to establish an independent nation west of the Alleghenies. Wilkinson authorized Pike's explorations of the headwaters of the Mississippi and of the Arkansas Rivers. The popular assumption then, for a hundred and fifty years, has been that Pike was not an explorer and a loyal soldier, but the tool of Wilkinson, spying out the land and carrying secret orders aimed at establishing the new nation which both Wilkinson and Burr hoped to establish.

In getting together the materials for this book, I have carefully read through Pike's own journals of his two great explorations and all the greater part of his letters to both General Wilkinson and Secretary of War Henry Dearborn. The picture that emerges is that of a zealous, competent, determined soldier whose sin, if he had any at all, was that he was loyal to his commanding officer and the United States Army.

Other and more competent writers who have gone deeply into the story of Zebulon Pike have in recent years arrived at the same conclusion—namely that Pike, far from being disloyal to his country, was one of the few trustworthy officers in an army riddled with self-seeking men. Pike died for his country on the field of battle at the age of thirty-four and I expect that as the years pass he will take his proper place in the annals of American exploration. That place will be beside the revered names of Lewis and Clark.

This, however, is not a book pleading a special cause. I have merely tried to put down Pike's story as it can be gained from

v

his own writings and the writings of those who knew him. But I must confess to a few of those liberties which a biographer working from incomplete material must take. One instance will suffice as an illustration: Pike himself asserted that he was present at the Battle of Fallen Timbers as a youth of fifteen, in the army of Anthony Wayne. There is no evidence to the contrary, though some have doubted that he was present at the battle. I feel entitled to take Pike's own word for it. The details of his part in the battle and his contact with Wayne, I plainly confess I have had to fabricate. There is no record beyond his own bald statement that he was there.

Have I the right to imagine conversations between a fifteen-year-old boy and "Mad" Anthony Wayne? I think so. Pike's father was a veteran of the Revolutionary War and had fought under Wayne's command. It would be natural that the father would ask the General to keep an eye on his young son. It would be natural that they should exchange a few words on the eve of battle. Generals are human and "Mad" Anthony Wayne was one of the most human of generals. As for the details of the battle itself, I have faithfully followed the record.

One final word. Pike has been criticized for being so poorly prepared for the rigorous winters he and his men endured in the headwaters of the Mississippi and in the front range of the Rockies. The critics ignore the fact that he was going into unexplored territory, that he did not know how long he would be upon his journey, and that winter supplies for a young lieutenant were hardly to be obtained. Pike has also been criticized as incompetent for losing his way in the Rockies. But these are the criticisms of people who have never been in a vast mountain chain, who have never seen ridge tumbling upon ridge, peak upon peak, and valley upon valley. It is one thing to look at a map of mountains. It is another thing to penetrate mountains which are unexplored, unnamed, and unpopulated. The traveler today, driving through the Rockies, in midwinter, has only to stop his car, climb two ridges on foot, and he will find himself as hopelessly lost as did Zebulon Pike.

Contents

CHAPTER ONE

Indian Attack

T HE INDIANS ATTACKED just before dawn. They were Miamies and Shawnees, and they had gathered during the night in the thick forest that surrounded the little American encampment on the Wabash. There were thousands of warriors well armed with guns and knives and tomahawks whose steel blades had been made in Europe. They waited until the poorly drilled band of militiamen under General St. Clair had been paraded by the light of lanterns and torches in the clearing and had been dismissed. And then, as the companies of militia trooped off to their tents and huts and put their muskets away, the forest around them suddenly blazed with gunshot and the quiet of the predawn air was shattered by the war cries of the redmen.

Under the hail of bullets men stumbled to the ground in heaps, and panic spread through them. Some threw down their muskets and ran into the few log buildings of the encampment. Some broke for the forests to the rear. The officers tried to rally the panicked men, but they were not regular soldiers. They were drifters and small farmers and packmen and greenhorns, untrained in Indian fighting and weary of frontier living and the strain of being forever on the alert for just such an attack as this. They were in the grip of terror and could think only of their own safety.

Captain Zebulon Pike, Senior, a veteran of the Revolutionary War, who had withstood the British charge at the Battle of Long Island and had seen Cornwallis surrender at Yorktown six years later, did his best to rally his company. They had paraded closer to the wall of the forest than the rest of the troops and so, in the first few minutes, received the heaviest of the Indian fire.

"Form a square!" he roared. "Form a square!" Perhaps a third of his company had enough discipline to obey his orders. They formed some kind of a line and blazed back at the dark forest from which the fire had come. They heard their rounds flickering through the leaves and twigs of the trees or smacking with a flat thud into the trunks. But their fire was wasted for the Indians were well hidden among the trees and in the underbrush. And then there came another volley and the handful of men who in all the confusion had made what stand they could was torn like a rag in the wind by the fusillade of bullets.

General Richard Butler, who had commanded the frontiersmen of Pennsylvania during the Revolutionary War under "Mad" Anthony Wayne, toppled from his horse, a bullet through his arm and his chest.

"For God's sake, Pike," he cried, "give me a brace of loaded pistols. I am done but would die fighting."

Pike gave the general his own pistols and turned again to his men. When he paraded his company a few minutes before, there had been a hundred of them. Now there were scarcely twenty. He snatched up a musket from a dead soldier and put himself before his men, between them and the Indians.

"Down!" he cried. "On your bellies. And don't fire until you have a target." The men obeyed and the next volley from the Shawnees whistled over their heads. It found a target, however, for the center of the encampment was now a mob of panicked militiamen and among them were their wives and children, the women looking for their husbands and the men looking for their families who had come on garrison duty with them. The women shrieked and the children screamed, and above these cries and the thunder of the muskets came the doglike howl of the Shawnee war cry.

Into this melee of people, the Shawnees were now firing from all sides, still remaining in the forest. Some of the other officers, all of whom were of the regular army, had by now managed to get a few bands of militiamen to make a stand. But they were hampered by the mob of others who got between them and the Indians. It was plain that what lay ahead was slaughter.

Gradually a semblance of order was restored, though the slaughter continued. The women and children were herded into a log cabin which served as a temporary barracks. Some of the militiamen were rallied to form a square in the encampment. But their position was hopeless. There was no time to put up earthworks to protect themselves. They lay or knelt on the ground, and the Shawnees, finding them difficult targets in this position, climbed into the trees to pour their fire down on them from above. It was plain that they must retreat and make their way as best they could to Fort Jefferson, the nearest outpost, which was thirty miles away through the forest.

By now it was light and groups of the Shawnees were making raids into the clearing, swooping down on the wounded and dragging them screaming into the forest where they were butchered. The firing was slacker from the east and General St. Clair gave orders to move off in that direction.

The orders were no sooner given than the demoralized militiamen made a scramble for the eastern wall of the forest. The Indians saw them going and with a wild shout poured out of the forest into the clearing. Captain Pike tried to hold them off with his men, but they poured down upon them doing terrible work with their tomahawks and knives. His own company stayed together and fought their way out, reloading and firing as they went. Once Pike found himself surrounded by Shawnees. He was not a big man, but he was a trained fighting man. It was not the first time he had been cut off from his men and had fought his way out. He flung his musket into the face of one warrior and then ran him through with his sword. The sword was a weapon he knew how to use well, and with it, he cut a path for himself through to the rear.

He caught one glimpse of General Butler in the mêlée. The old veteran of the Revolutionary War, who had campaigned side by side with General Washington and been with him through the dark days at Valley Forge, was dead. There was a cluster of savages around him engaged in frightful butchery of the corpse. It was a terrible way for such a hero to die, but it was a soldier's death and what a soldier must expect.

Soldiers. That was what the country needed. Soldiers. Not a mob of militia, recruited from the dregs of the frontier. Pike was fiercely angry that the penny-scraping Congress refused to garrison the frontier with regular troops, and so brave men died and settlers were murdered by the Indians with impunity.

By now Pike had gained the forest with his men and told them to make their way to Fort Jefferson. The rest of the garrison was fleeing, but there were very few women among them. The women had been left to fend for themselves, and Pike later discovered that of two hundred women who had been with the garrison, only three survived the massacre.

Pike himself ran for perhaps a quarter of a mile with his company, and then, with the screams of the Shawnees coming closer, for they had turned from their butchery in the clearing to chase the remnant of the garrison through the forest, his legs began to cramp. His legs were weak—a result of the privations he had suffered during the Revolutionary War. Now the muscles of his calves and thighs tightened, and he could do no more than hobble along. He could not go any faster. He had been fighting for four hours and was exhausted. He hobbled to the foot of a big pine and sat down on a log. He had picked up a pistol and loaded it. When the Shawnees came, they would get one last shot from him as they had had one last shot from General Richard Butler.

A man on horseback galloped out of the underbrush toward him, and he recognized Dr. Ellison, the surgeon of his regiment. He had a boy of six on the pommel of his saddle and the boy's eyes were glazed with terror at the terrible things he had seen.

"For God's sake, Pike, run!" cried the surgeon. "The Shawnees are right behind me. I have just snatched this lad out of their hands."

"Go on and save the boy," shouted Pike. "I can go no more. My legs have cramped, and I cannot move them."

"Up man," cried the surgeon. "Grab the horse's mane."

He reached down and took Pike by the arm and hauled him to his feet. Pike got a handful of the horse's mane and the surgeon dug his spurs into the animal's flanks. The horse plunged forward dragging Pike with it. He was compelled now to move his legs and he trotted along beside the horse, listening to the whimpering of the boy. His heart was black with anger. After three miles the Indians gave up the pursuit and Pike, Ellison, and the boy made their way to Fort Jefferson.

This massacre of the American garrison on the shores of the Wabash had taken place on November 4, 1791. A full report was sent by General St. Clair to President Washington. St. Clair spared no details. He reported how the militia had broken and run at the first attack and the women had fought better than the men. He related how General Richard Butler had died, how children had been butchered by the savages, and how men and women who had been taken prisoner had been tortured to death.

The details of the massacre were given to the Congress. President Washington stressed that the lesson was the same as they had learned during the early days of the Revolutionary War—the country must have a trained professional army to guard its frontiers. Reliance on militiamen, drawing pay only when on active service, receiving little training, and resentful of discipline, was military foolishness. The eastern seaboard was safe from attack. But the western frontier was a land of terror.

The Indians, elated by the success of their massacre, were butchering settlers all through the Ohio Territory. A professional army was needed to guard these frontiers and make the land safe for settlement by Americans. There must be chains of forts up and down the western rivers, within easy march of each other. And the forts must be garrisoned by men whose sole occupation and training was that of a soldier.

In the shame of the Indian victory, Congress put aside its fears of a standing army and voted money to train and equip a force of five thousand officers and men for the western frontier. This was the first move toward the opening up of the American west. The years ahead would see the establishment of a chain of military forts to guard settlers across the prairies, and in the terrible dry deserts of Arizona, and up into the mountains and forests of Oregon and Washington, and to the coasts of California.

But at this time the frontier had not yet advanced beyond the Mississippi-Missouri river system. Western Pennsylvania was still a wilderness, and Ohio was Indian Territory. The Shawnee, Sauk-Fox, Kickapoo, Wyandot, Cocktaw, and Huron Indian tribes controlled the lands from the lower Mississippi to the Great Lakes. Into these lands it was inevitable that the people of the United States, a nation scarcely ten years old, must penetrate. But they could not do so without the protection of an army; for the British in the north and the Spanish in the south spurred on the Indians to attack the settlers.

The job was one for soldiers, and at that time, and for many years to come, there was no other profession held in such general contempt as that of a soldier. Soldiers, the people felt, were ne'er-do-wells—men who could not succeed in any other walk of life. They were swearers and hard drinkers and gamblers, not fit company for decent folk.

But Captain Zebulon Pike, Senior, was a soldier, and he knew otherwise. So when the new western army was formed and the command given by President Washington to "Mad" Anthony Wayne, the Captain determined that his son would be a soldier too.

The boy was fourteen at the time, and not physically strong. Yet within him there was an inner strength, a quiet, unwavering determination that was as strong and unmovable as a mountain.

Captain Pike's son was also named Zebulon—Zebulon Montgomery Pike. And before he died, he was to give his name to a mountain—Pike's Peak—the magnificent white silent mountain of Colorado which was the symbol of the strength he contained in his own frail frame.

CHAPTER TWO

Young Soldier

CHAPTER TWO

ZEBULON MONTGOMERY PIKE had to wait until he was fifteen before he could legally join the United States Army, but before he put on his uniform for the first time, he was already much of a soldier. He knew all the drill of an infantry man—knew how to read maps and how to deploy troops and how to use cavalry in support of infantry. He had learned these things from his father, who had told him again and again the stories of the major battles of the Revolutionary War.

Zebulon was born in Lamington (then called Lamberton), in Somerset County, New Jersey. His family had a long history of tuberculosis, and although Zeb had several brothers and sisters, only two brothers and one sister survived childhood. The rest died of the disease. Of these George, a younger brother who went to West Point died of tuberculosis when he was nineteen. The other brother,

James, also younger than Zebulon, lived to be over seventy. But all his life he was an invalid, incapable of supporting his family of eight children. Zebulon's surviving sister, Maria, did not escape the scourge. She married a lawyer, Thomas Wardell, who soon after died. Then she married Anderson Gage. Gage, though healthy at the time of his marriage, contracted tuberculosis soon afterward, perhaps from his wife, who seems to have been a carrier. Like his brother-in-law James, he lingered on as an invalid, unable to support his wife and children. Tuberculosis dogged all the Pikes, and although Zebulon was not afflicted, the stamp of the disease seemed reflected in his light bones and small frame.

The family moved time and again after Zebulon's birth. They went from one small farm to another, and consequently Zebulon got little formal schooling. From New Jersey, the family went to eastern Pennsylvania and then further west. Finally the elder Pike, who had been honorably discharged from the army at the close of the Revolutionary War, joined the Pennsylvania militia in the Indian wars and so found his way back into the regular army. His talk was all the time of soldiering, and Zebulon early decided that the army was the only life for him.

One thing his father always stressed—discipline. Discipline was the very essence of soldiering. Discipline must be drilled so thoroughly into men that they would rather face death than disobey an order and disgrace their regiment.

"Everybody has about the same amount of courage," the elder Pike would say. "All else being equal, it's discipline that makes the difference between victory and defeat."

When young Zebulon joined "Mad" Anthony Wayne's western army, which had been given the name of The Legion, at Fort Washington, outside the village of

Cincinnati on the Ohio River, he was prepared for a hard life, but some of the disciplinary measures taken shocked him at first.

He saw men ducked in the icy waters of the Ohio in midwinter for appearing on parade improperly dressed. He saw them flogged for more serious offenses and more than once was compelled to witness a soldier writhing under a hundred lashes administered as punishment for striking an officer or for selling his musket or some other part of his equipment. He hated this kind of disciplinary action, but he knew that it was necessary.

Only the poorest kind of men, without principles of any sort, were willing to enlist in the regular army. They were men addicted to drinking and stealing and fighting, and they had to be made into soldiers. Some were wanted on a dozen charges in the eastern states, and so had fled to the frontier to escape trial and punishment. Since there was a belief that a man was safe from the law if he wore an army uniform, the army was filled with the outcasts of the east. And this was to be the force which must break the growing power of the Indians, supported as they were by both the British and French.

When he was not much more than fifteen years old, young Zeb Pike was put in charge of a squad of these ruffians in his father's company at Fort Washington.

"Make soldiers out of them, Zeb," his father said when he handed over to him command of the squad. And this the boy determined to do. At first the men thought it would be easy to fool him. At target practice they fired their rounds wildly and complained that their muskets were inaccurate.

Zeb took the musket from one of his men and brought down a flying pigeon with it. "If you drank less whisky, you'd shoot better," he said, handing the gun back to the man.

He was uncompromising about dress. Although Fort Washington was in the wilderness, and around it to north, south, and west there was nothing but gloomy tangled forests, through which the only roadways were the rivers, he wanted his men dressed for parade as if they were back in New York or New Jersey. To raise money for gambling or drinking, his men would often sell their boots and wear moccasins on parade. Other officers tolerated this. But not young Zebulon Pike. Pike's men not only had to have their boots, but boots and leggings had to be clean. When he found a man on parade in moccasins, he stamped hard on the man's foot and the offender learned his lesson fast.

Soon the efficiency of Pike's squad was noticed by General James Wilkinson, who was in command at Fort Washington.

He was a big bluff man in his mid-forties; a soldier and trader and adventurer, ambitious for himself. He had served under Benedict Arnold at the storming of Quebec in the early days of the Revolutionary War and had been adjutant-general to General Horatio Gates. At the close of the Revolutionary War, seeking a quick fortune and contemptuous of the more settled eastern states, he had crossed the Alleghenies into the western frontier lands and settled on a large acreage near the falls of the Ohio River. He was a man of courage, but one who put himself before his country. What he saw in the western frontier was a splendid opportunity to advance his own fortunes if he played his cards right. Patriotism hardly entered his mind, though Zebulon was not aware of this.

Wilkinson then, seeing how Zeb Pike drilled his men and kept excellent discipline among them, invited the young officer to dinner at his quarters. Zeb was flattered to be the guest of a great hero of the Revolution, a man whose exploits stood in his eyes side by side with those of General Wayne himself.

"You are young for the army," Wilkinson said to Zebulon.

"Yes, sir," Zeb replied. "But it is to be my profession. It has been my father's profession, and I can think of nothing better than to follow in his footsteps."

"My compliments on the discipline of your men," said Wilkinson. "It will not go unrewarded. I will bear you in mind should any opportunity for promotion present itself. How old are you?"

"Fifteen," replied Zebulon.

"Fifteen, eh? I myself was eighteen at the storming of Quebec in '75. I saw the great Montgomery fall, cut down by musket balls as we entered the breach—he ahead of us all."

"It was for him that I was given my middle name," said Zebulon. "He died for his country. There is no better death."

The general was touched, remembering the burning patriotism of his youth. For a moment he remembered the thrill of the charge and the shouts of "Liberty or Death," and the toasts that had been drunk to fallen comrades and to perdition to the king. He turned his head away from the eager, admiring look of the young officer before him and said shortly, "Yes. He died for his country. He died—too young. I trust you will not share his fate." There was an awkward silence, and then the general added, "Count me your friend if I can be of service to you."

Back in his quarters Zeb Pike was elated to have won the favor of the famous General Wilkinson. He determined that he would never be found wanting in his duty and looked forward eagerly to the day when the army would set out to meet the Indians on the field of battle.

But others at Fort Washington and in Cincinnati scoffed openly at the army's prospects. The terrible defeat that had been inflicted on General St. Clair had completely shaken the faith of the frontier people in the ability of the army to protect them from the Indians. Some said that the government in the eastern states was not interested in protecting them. They were westerners—people who had chosen to live west of the Alleghenies—and they had few ties in common with the people of the eastern states. They felt that neither the Congress nor the President cared much about what happened to them.

Furthermore, it was known that the Congress wanted to make peace with the Indians. Indeed, three peace commissioners had been sent to deal with the Shawnee, Choctaw, and Miami tribes. Two of them were murdered. The third, prudently, did not venture far into Indian territory. An approach to the Indians was made through British intermediaries.

At this the frontiersmen were openly contemptuous. They well knew that the British were arming the Indians and encouraging them to attack the American settlements. Indeed, Zebulon Pike learned that on the frontier there was so little faith in Congress and the protection of the army that many frontiersmen were prepared to become British or Spanish subjects, if that would bring an end to the Indian attacks on their little farms.

He chafed now at the delay in getting the punitive expedition against the Indian tribes under way. He had expected that in a month—two at the most—General Wayne would lead his men against the Indians. But month followed month, and still the army did not move. The people of the frontier said that this was because the officers were afraid of the Indians.

It was well over a year before General Wayne was prepared to move, and he had spent the interim in thoroughly drilling his men. He wanted them so disciplined that it would be second nature to them to obey commands. He wanted such a spirit drilled into his men that they would never be thrown into confusion by the wild attacks of the Indians. He wanted them to fire only when told; to charge only when told; to retreat only when told. Wayne knew that the defeat St. Clair had suffered—a greater defeat than that sustained by the British General Braddock in the French and Indian Wars—had been the result of the lack of discipline among his men. And so he drilled them and disciplined them until he had forged a military weapon that he believed was proof against surprise or panic.

Then in the spring of 1794 General Wayne ordered his army into the hostile Indian territory to the north. His objective was a large Indian settlement near the Maumee River, a hundred and fifty miles away, where Chief Little Turtle, together with Chiefs Blue Jacket and Tecumseh, had assembled a large band of warriors.

The journey north took the better part of three months. Wayne was in no hurry. His men had for months been trained behind the security of their fort. He wanted them to get accustomed to the boding solitudes of the forest, to the nights of utter blackness when moon and starlight were cut off by the interlocking branches of the trees, to the nerve-wracking howls of hunting wolves, and the possibility at all times of a sudden attack by a band of Indian braves.

He was determined also not to make the mistake of traveling ahead of his supplies. The men marched beside the creaking ox-drawn wagons, each wagon escorted by

its own squad of soldiers. In some places the forest was so
thick that several days had to be spent cutting down trees
so that the wagons could move ahead. Rivers and creeks
had to be forded, sometimes by day and sometimes by
night. The hours before dusk and before dawn were the
hours of danger. Every man stood to arms at these times,
waiting, with the quiet forest around, for an Indian attack.

Some of Wayne's officers complained at the slow progress
of the army. "The Indians will be enormously reinforced
by the time we reach their settlement," they said. "We
should swoop down on them now and destroy them while
we can and discourage others from joining."

Zeb Pike was present when this view was expressed over
the campfire in the wilderness, and he heard Wayne's reply.

"Gentlemen," said Wayne, clear enough for the young
officers to hear, "I trust that the Indians are gathered in
the greatest possible force when we meet them. I hope
that we are outnumbered and that warriors from all the
tribes of the Northwest are represented in the Indian
army. For only by a victory against an overwhelming force
of Indians can we wipe out the defeat of General St. Clair
and make the lands west of the Alleghenies safe for settlers.
The task before us is not merely one of winning a battle.
It is one of securing such respect from the Indians that
there will be an end to the threat of Indian wars in these
parts.

"The future of our country depends on the result of the
present expedition. Defeated, our nation will be confined
to the lands east of the Alleghenies. Victorious, the United
States can and will expand to the shores of the Pacific.
The issue rests with us."

Wayne had risen to make this little address and, in the

light of the campfire, presented a splendid figure in his
full uniform, with his white wig neatly powdered.

He stood looking now beyond the campfire and the
circle of officers seated around into the darkness of the
forest, as if he were about to address the shadows among
the trees.

"We are not unaccompanied as we move through the
wilderness, gentlemen," he continued. "Moving with us,
although invisible to us, are scouts of the Indian army.
They watch us night and day. They have exact details of
our strength and armament and physical condition. They
are sending their reports back to Little Turtle, their chief.
I am glad they are doing so and have given instructions
that they are not to be molested.

"I want Little Turtle to know the strength in which we
come and the depth of our determination. I have some
hope that he will cede these territories to us without bloodshed. I have seen enough of bloodshed to wish to avoid
more. But I will not flinch from battle, if battle is the
answer. And I believe I now command such men as will
not flinch either."

There was a pause when he had finished, and one of the
senior officers asked a question. "The place where Little
Turtle has gathered his army," he said, "is, as you know,
not far from Fort Miami—a British fort, though in American territory. I have heard that if the battle goes against
Little Turtle, the British regulars from the fort will re-
inforce him. Do you think this possible?"

"I cannot say one way or the other," replied General
Wayne. "We know that the British are behind the Indians
and have made promises of support. We know that they
have armed them. But whether they are willing, on behalf
of the Indians, to risk open warfare with the Army of the
United States is another matter." He paused and added

with a smile, "As you perhaps know, I am not unaccus-
tomed to fighting the British."

When he heard these replies from his general, Zebulon
Pike began to see the expedition in a new and more glori-
ous light. This was not only a punitive expedition, as he
had thought, but a campaign to win vast lands for the
United States. In the wilderness through which they now
marched, rich farmlands might some day appear, and
cities grow on the muddy scrub-entangled shores of the
rivers and creeks which they crossed or traveled along.

Whose land was it, anyway? he wondered. The British
and French had fought over it for years until, in the
French and Indian Wars, the British finally obtained
possession. But at the Treaty of Paris, concluding the
Revolutionary War, the British had ceded the land to the
new United States of America.

Yet the Spanish had vague claims to it, and the French
were active in it, and the British were using the Indians
to prevent America from claiming the land. Vaguely
Zebulon Pike began to suspect that the British had ceded
the land to the United States only to entangle the United
States in a war with France or Spain or with the Indian
tribes. The problem was more than he could cope with,
but, as they moved northward, the conviction grew in his
mind that to obtain sovereignty over the western territories, the United States would have to fight one or perhaps several European powers.

Two forts were constructed on the march north. They
went up fast, for they were built of logs; the ring of blades
on the trunks of trees sounded strange in the quiet air of
the forest. The axmen worked under a guard of soldiers.
The first of these forts was constructed on the site of the
massacre of St. Clair's army. Zebulon, directing his party
of men, found in the tangled undergrowth the skeletons

of those who had fallen in that terrible slaughter. Many
were skeletons of children. The fort was named, by General Wayne, Fort Recovery a name that would convey to
the Indians the purpose of his mission.

At this fort Wayne's army was reinforced by fifteen
hundred militiamen from Kentucky. These men looked
wilder than the Indians they were going to fight. Heavily
bearded, they ate with their hands, cutting their meat with
hunting knives. They were dressed in deerskins, and their
mission was one of personal vengeance for the death of
relatives and friends at the hands of the Indians. Parties
of them would go out on what they called "hunting expeditions." Sometimes they returned with game. Sometimes they brought back the scalp locks of Indians they
had killed. It was a matter of honor among them that
they wore their hair long so that, if they were killed, the
brave who killed them could take their scalps. A man with
a close-cropped head they reckoned a coward.

The second fort on the Maumee River was called Fort
Defiance.

Recovery and Defiance. General Wayne planted these
two words in the wilderness in the form of forts. At Fort
Defiance he sent some of the frontiersmen to Chief Little
Turtle, whose army now lay not many miles ahead down
the river, offering peace, but stating that he was prepared
for war if the Indians were not ready to accept the sovereignty of the United States of America and leave the
American settlers in peace.

The reply he got back was unsatisfactory. Little Turtle
would give no guarantees. His attitude was contemptuous.
He believed he could deal with the army of General
Wayne as he had dealt with the army of General St. Clair.

General Wayne was not surprised at the defiance of the
Indians. He had received news that Lord Dorchester,

governor-general of Canada, had addressed a large meeting
of the Indians and assured them that the British would
help them eject the American settlers. He had even sent
a column of Redcoats down to Fort Miami to lend weight
to his words.

When his emissaries returned, General Wayne called his
officers together.

"Gentlemen," he said, "it must be war, And I want no
indecisive battle fought. Either the Indian host must be
destroyed or we must be destroyed. Anything less will
serve no purpose."

He then laid down his plans.

Little Turtle, Blue Jacket, and Tecumseh had their
army of braves encamped on top of a long hill where a
tornado a few years before had broken down a swathe of
trees nearly two miles long. These trees formed a natural
breastwork behind which the Indians intended to fight.
One side of the Indian line was protected by a river, but
there was no protection for the other side. However, between the breastwork of fallen trees and the river there
was a small gap.

"I propose to put our horses' hooves on their moccasins,"
said General Wayne. "The cavalry will be split into two
parties, one to go around their line on the landward side
and take them in the flank and the rear; the other to get
through the gap between their breastworks and the river
and attack them from that side. The infantry will storm
the breastworks from the front—with the bayonet."

He paused to let the significance of this plan sink in.

"There is to be no halting of the line, once the order to
charge is given," he said. "And no firing. We can expect the Indians to fire upon us from behind their breastwork as we charge forward. But I do not want that fire
returned. Speed will be of the essence. It takes, as you

know, five minutes to reload a musket. In the five minutes from the first discharge of the enemy, we must be over the breastwork and among them with the bayonet. Thereafter it will be bayonet against tomahawk—the 'long knife' against the war ax. I shall, of course, lead the charge. And I shall carry only my sword. I wish you luck, gentlemen."

And with that General Wayne closed the conference.

Battle for the Northwest

CHAPTER THREE

THE ATTACK WAS LAUNCHED the following day—the twentieth of August, 1793. It was a day of wind and rain, the landscape darkened by huge cloud masses which brooded over the field of battle. Gusts of wind whipped the rank grass and brush through which General Wayne's army marched in three columns toward the entrenched hordes of Indians, who numbered two thousand warriors of several tribes. At times these gusts were so heavy that the men staggered as they pressed forward into the storm, and the waters of the River Maumee were lashed with waves by the fury of the gale.

The weather itself was enough to make the hearts of the attackers quail. And when they came in sight of the Indian entrenchment, there were many who felt the task before them was impossible and their lives were to be thrown uselessly away.

They saw a huge wall of trees, trunks piled upon trunks, and any gaps between them filled by an impenetrable tangle of branches. This tree wall was two miles long and on the top of a small hill. They must advance up the hill to get to the trees and then clamber over these to reach the enemy. And during all this they would be under fire from the Indians.

Despite their discipline, the men of Zebulon Pike's little squad, which was in the forefront of the American line, murmured that the task was impossible. They had been told that they were not to fire, but were to go forward with the bayonet. But what could the bayonet do against that huge log wall that confronted them?

Suddenly a storm of shot came from the breastwork of fallen trees and the tall grass which grew at the foot of the hill. Several men jerked back or spun around and fell on the muddy ground. The others brought their muskets to the firing position.

"No firing," shouted Zebulon Pike. "I'll cut down the first man who looses a round." The men of his company knew that he meant what he said and withheld their fire.

Off to the right a drum rolled, the tattoo heard above the howling of the wind and the lashing of the rain. Then came several clear notes on a bugle.

It was the signal to form into the line of charge. The rattle of the drums and the shrill notes of the bugle, sounds with which the men were thoroughly familiar, served to restore their nerve.

The result of months of drilling asserted itself, and the men filed off, shoulder to shoulder, into two lines with one flank on the river and the other stretching to the end of the Indian position. The line was thin, and there were gaps of six or seven feet between each man. But this wide spacing was an advantage, for when the next volley came from the Indians, no massed target was presented and their marksmanship was so bad that few were hit.

General Wayne, accompanied by a small group of officers, rode down the American line. As he came abreast of the officer of each company, he heard the report, "All present and correct." There was a smile of satisfaction on his face as he passed Zeb's position.

"Present and correct, sir," said Zeb.

Wayne nodded, eying the youngster who at fifteen was experiencing his first battle before he had even experienced his first shave.

"Who is that young fellow?" he inquired of an aide.

"Zebulon Pike, Captain Pike's son," was the reply.

"Oh, yes." The general hesitated a moment, staring at Zeb, who was afraid that he would be sent to the rear because of his youth. Then, with a nod, Wayne passed on and the crisis was over.

When Wayne had made his inspection, word was passed along the line that the front line alone was to charge on the signal. The rear line would remain in reserve and storm forward once the front line had gained a foothold on the breastwork.

Then once again the drums rolled and the bugles blared out the notes of the charge. To the beat of the drums the front line stepped off toward the Indian works, General Wayne riding ahead slowly on his horse. The men marked time to the tattoo of the drums, and as this sound quickened, they moved from a slow walk, to a brisk walk, to a trot. Then, at a final flourish from the bugles, they broke into a run, crouching low with their rifles—the long bayonets at the end—held before them. The Indians fired a further volley before the American line gained the foot of the hill, but without effect. Zeb scrambled up the hill and got to the log wall. He was climbing the logs when a brave appeared on the parapet above and fired directly at him. He heard the ball sing past his head, heaved himself upward, and, using his rifle as a club, toppled the brave back into the tangle of branches behind the tree trunks.

Suddenly the air was filled with the terrible shrieking of the Indians as they howled their war cries. A Choctaw brave, naked except for a loin cloth and painted with designs to make him invulnerable against his enemies, leaped at Zeb, his tomahawk raised. The boy jabbed his bayonet into the shoulder of the warrior, and the two went down together, Zeb knocked off his feet by the weight of the redman. He was up in a second, stabbed twice with the bayonet in vicious jerks, and moved on.

It seemed to Zebulon that for the next half hour he was living a nightmare. No sooner had he dealt with one enemy than there was another upon him. Beyond the wall of fallen trees, the forest grew so thick that there was little light and all was made more obscure by the smoke from the Indians' muskets.

At times he was quite alone, with the sounds of battle all around him, but no one to be seen in the thickets through the battle smoke. Then two or even three braves would come into view out of the smoke and scrub, and a fierce little battle would break out, in which his own men, appearing as it were from nowhere, would join.

He had no idea how the battle was going. He did not know how many of his men had got over the embankment of trees.

Far away to the left, above the din of battle, Zeb heard the screams of the warriors, the shouts of the soldiers, the discharge of muskets, and the thin scream of a bugle sounding the charge for cavalry. That meant that the American cavalry had swept around the flank of the Indian position and would probably take the Indians in the rear.

Suddenly he came upon a clearing in the forest with a high rock in its center. The clearing was full of warriors who had gathered there on their flight to the rear. One of their chiefs stood upon the rock shouting to them. Zeb, who had spent the greater part of his life on the frontier, caught some of the words. The chief was telling the braves that they were to stand firm and that the Great Spirit would make them strong and invulnerable to the Long Knives.

Almost as if to confirm the chieftain's promise, the heavy clouds overhead broke and a shaft of sunlight came down into the clearing, for a moment illuminating the splendid figure of the Indian chief.

Zeb loaded his rifle and took careful aim. Before he could press the trigger, the sunlight was gone and the clearing was plunged into gloom once more. In the darkness he pressed the trigger and at the same moment several other shots rang out. The chieftain pitched forward off the rock, dead.

Panic immediately gripped the Indians. They ran screaming from the clearing, not even bothering to pick up the body of the brave chief who had tried to rally them.

Now the battle turned into a rout and a massacre. Pushing forward after the Indians through the woods, Zeb found branches and leaves and grass stained with the blood of the fleeting warriors. No quarter was asked or given. The Indians were to be taught a terrible lesson, and no prisoners were to be taken.

The retreat led from the forest to a large clearing behind and beside the river. When Zeb got out of the thickets and trees, he saw the horde of warriors, their footsteps leaving a bloody trail on the ground, streaming toward a fort over which flew the Union Jack of Great Britain.

Fort Miami! The British would come to rescue the Indians and then the battle would really begin. But as the leaders of the Indian horde reached the huge gates of the British fort, the gates were swung shut in their faces. The British had no intention of becoming involved in a battle with United States troops. They had been bluffing all the time; now they left the Indians to be slaughtered outside the walls of the fort.

Some of the Indians tried to rally and make a stand. But against Wayne's disciplined troops, they had no chance. Wherever they gathered, the cavalry rode through them, cutting them down with their sabres. The warriors broke and ran, and their flight went on for seven miles before the bugle sounded the recall.

This was the Battle of Fallen Timbers, named for the breastwork that the Indians had used, and was the most important action of forty years of warfare against the Indians in the old Northwest. It was followed one year later by the Treaty of Greenville, in which the areas now forming the states of Ohio and Indiana were ceded by the Indian chiefs to the Americans for settling.

CHAPTER FOUR

Frontier Service

A<small>FTER THE BATTLE OF FALLEN TIMBERS</small> General Wayne did not forget the teen-age officer he had seen standing in the front line of the troops awaiting the signal to charge. He assigned Zebulon Pike to transport duty, bringing supplies overland and up the various rivers to the forts that had been constructed in the new territories.

This was work from which an unscrupulous officer could make plenty of profit, and many of them did just that. But young Pike soon won a reputation for complete honesty, and the stores he delivered to the forts were never as much as one barrel of pork short of what he was sent out with.

Before he was twenty Zebulon Pike was a veteran of wilderness travel. He spoke a dozen Indian dialects, knew how to navigate the huge keel boats through rapids and over shoals, and had learned how to survive in the wilder-

ness in midwinter. Most of all, he knew how to handle
men who were among the roughest ever to populate the
American frontier.

His method was to show that he could himself do anything he asked his men to do. When he sent out a hunting
party and the men returned without game, he would go
off himself with his rifle and return with a quarter of
venison to shame them. When they grumbled at the toil
of rowing the heavily laden keel boats upstream against
the flood, he would push a man aside and take his place
at the huge oar, rowing not for an hour or two hours but
for half a day. He still had the figure of a boy, but his
spirit was superhuman. Sometimes he lost his temper with
the men, and then they discovered a white heat of fury
in him that cowed them for days afterward.

One freezing winter morning, when the men had broken
camp and had boarded the boats that they were to take
up the Ohio, he found that most of them had crowded into
one of the bigger boats which was equipped with a sail.
In the small keelboats that had no sail and would have to
be rowed up the river there had to be nine men.

"Some of you man the smaller boats," Zeb shouted from
the bank. But the men remained huddled in the big boat,
refusing to face a day's toil at the oars. He repeated the
order twice but without effect. Then he lost his temper.

"By thunder," he shouted, "I'll teach you to move when
I tell you." Whirling about, he grabbed flaming brands
from the fire ashore and flung them into the men huddled
in the big keel boat. With cries of alarm and pain they
jumped out of the boat into the river and climbed into
the smaller boats. They rowed the rest of the day in wet
clothing for their disobedience.

For the next several years young Zeb Pike was employed
taking goods by boat down the Ohio and the Mississippi to

the various forts strung along the rivers. His father was stationed at Fort Massac, which was on the north bank of the Ohio about forty miles from its juncture with the Mississippi, so Zebulon saw him frequently. In 1799, because of his hard work and honesty and the discipline he maintained among his men, he was promoted to second lieutenant and then to full lieutenant. Then he was put in charge of the construction of a new fort, a few miles below Fort Massac.

The man who singled him out for this job was General James Wilkinson, whom he had first met in the months of training before the Battle of Fallen Timbers. Wilkinson had not forgotten the keen young officer whose well-disciplined troops had attracted his attention. He made Pike adjutant of the corps situated at the new fort, which was called Wilkinsonville. More forts were to be constructed down the Mississippi, and Wilkinsonville, on the Ohio, was a receiving center for the men who would be stationed at the new fort. Zebulon Pike was kept busy in a hundred ways—drill three times a week, all the records of the fort to be kept, men to be provisioned and dispatched to their destinations, keel boats to be loaded and unloaded, and so on.

The free moments he had he devoted to his education. He had been raised with but the scantiest schooling. His mother had taught him to read and write and calculate. Beyond that he had had no education. He taught himself the rudiments of surveying, of geometry, and of astronomy. Books were hard to come by on the frontier, but there was one he got hold of in his youth and kept with him throughout his life. It became his bible and was entitled *The Economy of Human Life.* The author was Robert Dodsley—a man who had at one time been a footman in the service of an English nobleman, but who had

by his own efforts established one of the most famous publishing houses in England. It was Dodsley who encouraged
Dr. Samuel Johnson to compile his dictionary and who
published it later. Some of the greatest writers in England
had their works published by the former footman who put
down his plan for self-improvement in the book that he
called "The Economy of Human Life."

One precept was emphasized again and again in this
book: Learn all you can; there is no such thing as useless
knowledge. When he first came upon these words, Zebulon
Pike was greatly impressed by them and determined to
act on them. Accordingly, he taught himself all he could.

During his trips supplying the forts on the Ohio River,
Zebulon had time to visit some of the planters whose es-
tates lay on the river's banks. He never failed to stop at
one plantation—Sugar Grove—which was fifteen miles
below Cincinnati and owned by Captain John Brown.
There was a good social reason for the stops here, for
Captain Brown was the brother of Zebulon's mother. But
another reason presented itself in Captain Brown's dark-
haired and pretty daughter Clarissa. She was his partner
at dances held in the plantation house. Sometimes they
walked by the river together, slipping away from the rest
of the party. It was not long before they were deeply in
love, but Captain Brown opposed the match.

"A soldier for my daughter's husband, sir?" he said when
Zeb asked for Clarissa's hand. "I cannot agree to it. What
is your future? Garrison duty on the frontier, small pay
and few promotions. I want more than that for my
daughter."

Clarissa had anticipated her father's reaction. Now she
showed that she had just as much spirit as he. She and
Zebulon eloped to Cincinnati and were married over her

father's protests. The marriage brought about a breach between the Brown and Pike families, and Zebulon was not welcome at his father-in-law's estate afterward.

Meanwhile a great change had quietly taken place in the lands west of the Mississippi. Previously owned by Spain, they had been ceded by Spain to France in 1800. The reason was simple. The Spanish, nervous about the expansion of the United States of America through the lands east of the great river, were fearful that at some time the Americans might dispute the ownership of the territories west of the Mississippi.

Spain decided to place a buffer state between herself and the United States. She ceded the land west of the Mississippi to France. If the Americans were going to go to war with anyone over these lands, it would be with France.

When news of this vast exchange of territory came to Zebulon Pike, he decided to study French. He set himself to the task, aided by his wife who spoke French well.

His fellow officers laughed at his studies, but one officer took an interest in young Lieutenant Pike and dropped in on him occasionally. His name was Meriwether Lewis. Both were professional army men and talked about their future.

"Some day I would like to explore the Mississippi River northward to its source," said Zeb.

"Some day I would like to explore the Missouri westward and perhaps reach the Pacific," said Lewis.

They both laughed. It seemed impossible that two young officers serving on the frontier would ever get such vital assignments. And yet in his heart each held on to the hope that he would.

CHAPTER FIVE

North by Keelboat

U NKNOWN TO ZEBULON PIKE, frontier soldier and student of languages, negotiations were already taking place in France which were not only to shape his destiny but enormously alter the destiny of the United States of America.

As soon as news was received in Washington that Spain had ceded vast territories west of the Mississippi to France, including the port of New Orleans at the mouth of the great river, Secretary of State Madison instructed the United States minister in Paris, Robert R. Livingston, to negotiate for the sale of these lands to America.

The Spanish, under pressure from the United States, had granted Americans the right to send their goods down the Mississippi to be exported from the port of New Orleans. It was critical that France grant the same right, for without the use of this great waterway for the export

and import of goods, all American farming and industry
west of the Alleghenies would be strangled. These negotiations continued for months.

They were stupendously successful, and they proved
to be the greatest event in American history, other than the
winning of the Revolutionary War. In return for the sum
of $27,267,622 Napoleon sold to the United States a vast
territory west of the Mississippi covering an area of nearly
530,000,000 acres. The price worked out at about four
cents an acre!

The boundaries of the area, known as the Louisiana
Purchase, were only loosely set. Three countries were
really involved, for the French had obtained the land only
three years previously from the Spanish and had not
exactly defined it. The French had got out of the situation,
leaving the United States and Spain once more confronting
each other on the American continent and by no means
agreed as to where their respective territories ended.

One thing was certain, however. New Orleans was now
an American city. The area around it was quickly organized into the Territory of Orleans, and a governor was
appointed to handle its affairs. This territory constituted
the lower half of the famed Louisiana Purchase. The
upper half, called Upper Louisiana, or just Louisiana, embraced what were to become the states of Missouri, Iowa,
Wisconsin, Minnesota, North and South Dakota, Nebraska,
Kansas, part of Colorado, Wyoming, Montana, Idaho,
and Washington. The United States believed that it also
embraced the present state of Oregon, but this was later
agreed to be an error.

In any case, it was essential that such a huge new territory be explored and mapped. To this end Zebulon Pike's
friend, Meriwether Lewis, was sent with William Clark

by President Thomas Jefferson to explore the new territory overland to the Pacific.

A few months later Zebulon Pike, then commanding the frontier post of Kaskaskia in Illinois, near the Mississippi, received orders from General James Wilkinson to report to St. Louis. When young Lieutenant Pike presented himself at his commander-in-chief's office in St. Louis, Wilkinson unrolled on a table a map whose major features the young lieutenant recognized immediately. It was a map of the Mississippi River north of St. Louis.

"Beyond this point," said the general, putting a finger on the upper reaches of the Mississippi, "this map is mere guesswork. How deep the river is, how wide, in what direction it flows and at what speed, we do not know. We do not know what tribes live in these territories, whether the land can be cultivated or not; whether it is heavily timbered or desert land. We do not know the mountains or the hills in this area. It is all unexplored. All of this territory now belongs to the United States. I want you to take a party of men of your own choosing and go up the river—trace it to its source and map its flow. Are you willing to accept this assignment?"

"When do I start, sir?" said Zebulon quietly.

For a moment, General Wilkinson was surprised by Pike's quiet acceptance of so momentous an assignment.

"You have no questions to ask first?"

"None, sir," said Pike. "I have dreamed of such an assignment for a long time."

"You may start whenever you are ready," replied the General. "The earlier the better."

Zebulon wasted no time. He knew that Lewis and Clark had already set out on their western exploration to the Pacific. That the northern exploration of the Louisiana Purchase, to the unknown source of the Mississippi, had been entrusted to him, filled him with zeal. He threw himself into his preparations with such energy that even his own men, who were accustomed to his vigor, were surprised.

A few years earlier Zeb had brought his wife Clarissa and their daughter, also Clarissa, to St. Louis, where he found quarters for his small family. He now set about getting the flour, cornmeal, salted pork, gunpowder, salt, tobacco, calico, tents, blankets and other equipment he would require for his explorations. He bedevilled the quartermaster's office until he obtained a primitive kind of sextant for determining latitude and a thermometer with which to record temperatures of both the river and the air. These, together with a watch, which later proved to be grossly inaccurate, were all the scientific equipment he could lay hands on. He commissioned a seventy-foot keelboat and twenty soldiers to accompany him. Less than three weeks after receiving his orders, he was ready to get under way.

Before Pike set out, General Wilkinson gave him a letter outlining the task before him. He was to look for sites for two military forts to be erected for the protection of future settlers in the area. He was to obtain from the Indians permission to build these forts. He was to discover the names and sizes of the various tribes along the course of the river and the quantity of skins and furs they obtained each year. He was to note the direction of other rivers flowing into the Mississippi and find out how far the Mississippi could be navigated in boats. He was to take the latitude and longitude of the most notable places on the river and record islands and shoals and rapids.

He was to warn all traders in the area—British, French, or Spanish—that they were now operating in American territory and must obtain licenses from the United States

LAKE LEECH

FEB. 1, 1806 – PIKE REACHES LAKE LEECH

TREATY FOR 100,000 ACRES ON EITHER SIDE OF RIVER SIGNED WITH SIOUX

WISCONSIN

PIKE SAILS THROUGH RAPIDS IN HOWLING GALE

MINN. R.

MINNESOTA

MISSISSIPPI R.

DES MOINES R.

IOWA

FIRST CONTACT WITH SAC INDIANS IN SOUTHEAST IOWA

PIKE'S EXPLORATIONS ON THE MISSISSIPPI RIVER: 1805 – 1806

ILLINOIS

AUG. 9, 1805 – PIKE AND 20 MEN LEAVE ST. LOUIS WITH 70' KEEL BOAT

MISSOURI

ST. LOUIS

government and pay the regular taxes to the government. This latter was a very important point. The government suspected that British agents of the Hudson's Bay Company, or of its rival the Northwest Company, were buying huge quantities of beaver and fox furs from the Indians on American territory without paying a penny to the United States Government.

In those days the fur trade was as important a source of revenue as the oil industry was to become later. Pike was to put a stop to this illicit trade. His expedition then was not merely one of exploration. Quite as important was the task of establishing the authority of the United States in this new area. This authority had been established on paper with the Louisiana Purchase. Pike was to establish it in fact, planting the American flag in the northernmost reaches of the Louisiana Purchase. That would help to settle any arguments with the British in the future about the extent of the Purchase.

There was one note of warning in the order. Pike was to be careful to return early enough not to be caught in the northern winter.

On August 9, 1805, with his supplies and men aboard the seventy-foot keelboat, Zebulon Pike pushed off from the jetty in St. Louis and, with his big, square sail set, headed north up the "Father of Waters."

There was a pathetic little salute from the muskets of a company of soldiers assembled on the bank and a huzza from the motley crowd of trappers and traders who had come to see his departure.

Then, with a wind from the south, the keelboat lumbered steadily northward until, in a little while, it had disappeared around a bend of the mighty river.

CHAPTER SIX

Peril in the Rapids

CHAPTER SIX

ZEBULON PIKE had with him a sergeant, two corporals and seventeen privates when he set out up the Mississippi in his clumsy keelboat to find the source of the river. He had hand-picked his men and chosen only those who could swim and who had had previous experience along the rivers of the old Northwest Frontier. It was just as well that he had picked swimmers, for in August the Mississippi waters are low, and, almost from the start, the keelboat kept driving into sandbanks or ramming into dangerous submerged logs. The men then had to go over her side and push or haul her off, so that they spent a great deal of their time in the water.

The sergeant's name was Kennerman. He was a big, tough fellow, who could outrun, outjump and outfight any man in the squad; he prided himself on his ability to endure hardship. At the same time he was fond of music, and in the miscellaneous gear with which the keelboat was loaded, he had included a couple of fiddles and some flutes. He could scrape out a reel or a jig on the fiddle, stamping his big feet to keep time and occasionally letting out a high-pitched yell when it seemed to him that a particular passage required this embellishment. Zebulon got many a laugh out of his performances.

Almost as soon as the party set out, the weather turned foul. Rain pelted down into the muddy river, which in parts was two miles wide, obscuring the view. The keelboat floundered along through these rainstorms, making the best use of the wind, with a man up forward, warning the man at the tiller of islands or shoals that lay ahead.

But all the warnings could not prevent the keelboat from going aground at least once a day. Not long after they had set out, the huge boat, bowling along before a favorable wind, stopped suddenly with a thundering crash.

Zebulon was knocked to the deck by the impact. After he had scrambled to his feet, shouting to one of the men to lower the sail, he went below, to find the water pouring in through a staved plank. He quickly calked the leak with oakum—unraveled rope mixed with tar. He ordered the men over the side and went over with them. They heaved and pulled in an effort to get the keelboat off the submerged tree trunk she had run into, but all their efforts were useless. The boat was stuck fast on the trunk.

"Get a saw," shouted Zebulon, and Kennerman, clad only in his drawers, climbed back onto the boat and found one. The next couple of hours were spent sawing the submerged tree in two.

A branch of the tree had staved in one of the planks. As soon as the obstruction was cleared, the keelboat started to sink; it had been held above water by the submerged tree.

Zebulon got the sail up on her again and steered her for the bank, which was but a hundred yards away. With the water rising every second, he managed to beach her on a shoal near the bank. Then she was hauled over on her side, the broken plank removed, and a new one nailed in its place.

This was a serious mishap, occurring so early in the voyage, and all the more serious because a great part of the stores were drenched. A day was spent drying out the stores, and Zebulon sent one of the soldiers, Private John Sparks, out to hunt deer to augment their food supply.

Sparks went up the bank of the river about seven miles and saw a herd of deer on the other bank. The range was too great for his musket so he stripped down, wrapped the lock and pan of his musket in oilskin, strapped it to his shoulder, the butt end in the air, swam across the Mississippi, and shot one of the deer. He butchered his kill and waited for a while, thinking that the keelboat would soon be coming up the river to meet him. However, when, by midafternoon, there was still no sign of the boat, he put his musket on his back again, together with his clothes, and thus laden, swam seven miles downstream to rejoin his party.

"Reckon we'd better get that deer before the savages get it," was his comment to Zebulon as he pulled himself out of the water. Then he remembered Pike's insistence on his men being dressed in a soldierly manner at all times and realized that he was standing before his officer in his dripping and muddy underwear. He came swiftly to attention. "Had to leave me uniform to report back for duty, sir," he said. Zebulon burst out laughing at him.

They got the deer the next day, and Pike congratulated himself that the men were turning out to be of the strong character he had hoped for when he selected them.

The part of the Mississippi through which they were traveling was full of shoals and islands. The party averaged little more than twenty or thirty miles a day. Zebulon charted the positions of the islands, the direction of the river's flow, and its width. He made copious notes on the kind of land on either bank.

It was beautiful countryside. At times the banks were lined by groves of trees—cedar, locust, walnut, and oak. At times they found rich expanses of fertile meadowland, the grass on it so smooth that Zebulon was reminded of a beautifully kept lawn before some luxurious mansion. They met their first rapids at the confluence of the Des Moines River with the Mississippi in the extreme southeast corner of what is now the state of Iowa. They heard the roaring of the rapids for some time before they were in view, and Zebulon questioned the men, asking if any one had ascended them before.

No one had. Portaging was out of the question; even if they could carry their cargo along the bank past the rapids, they would still have to take their heavy boat through them.

The rapids proved to be eleven miles long, a series of rock ledges extending from shore to shore, interspersed by shoals and sandbanks. The water thundering over them was wild and white. Zebulon went ashore at the foot of the rapids on the east bank and found that there was a passage, though a poor one, through the first two ledges on that side. Back aboard, he eased the boat over to the eastern bank, and the men got out the huge poles with which they would work it upstream, for the sail would be useless to them.

The men started poling the boat, foot by foot, toward the first passage. Once they got the bluff bow of the keelboat into the passage, the work became very difficult. Here the flow of the water, confined to a small area, was very fast. Razor-sharp edges of rock jutted out on either side with the water boiling white around them. There were but a few feet between these ledges and the side of the boat; if the men faltered for a moment in poling the boat up through the gap, it would be taken by the river and smashed to splinters on the rocks.

The first fall proved to be the worst. The channel was very narrow, and the heavy boat could be driven up it only inch by inch. At times it stood still, the roaring water dragging it downstream as fast as the laboring men could push it up. There was no need for a man at the tiller, and Zebulon worked with his men at the poles. Little by little they drove the huge boat forward, the sweat streaming off their faces and the roaring of the water making it impossible for any orders to be heard.

But Zebulon had picked his men well. Each knew what he had to do and did it with a will, and after half an hour they got through the first passage into the comparatively calm water that lay beyond. There were several more falls to be got through, however, before the rapids would be passed. Suddenly out of the boiling water ahead appeared a number of canoes loaded with Indians. In the foremost a white man was standing, holding a United States flag. His canoe was soon alongside the keelboat.

"My name is Ewing," he shouted to Zeb. "William Ewing. We've come to help you."

Thirteen of the heaviest barrels were taken off the keelboat and transferred to the canoes. Two Indians came aboard to act as pilots and with their aid, the keelboat was at last got above the rapids. But only just in time, for it was dark when the last channel was cleared; without the aid of Ewing and the Indians, Zeb would have been caught by nightfall in the mist of the rapids.

Ewing, they learned, was an agent of the United States
Government sent to teach the Sac Indians agriculture. On
the following morning a council of chiefs of the tribe was
assembled. Dark-skinned, fierce, clad in loin cloths, and
decorated with strings of beads and medals, they squatted
around in a log house to hear what the "Chief of the Long
Knives" had to say. Zebulon's task was to tell them that
they were now under the protection of the United States
Government.

The speech he gave was one that he was to repeat many
times in his journey up the Mississippi. He said that their
Great White Father, the President of the United States,
wanted to become intimately acquainted with the different
nations of the Indians who had been committed to his
care and for this reason had sent him, Zeb, with his band
of young warriors, to meet the Indians.

He said that he had been ordered to pick sites for trading stations which would benefit the Indians and that he
would like their advice on whether the land nearby was
suitable. He had heard of the murder of a white man
further down the river, but he was assured that this was
not the doing of the members of the Sac nation, and he
had written to his General exonerating the Sacs. He
warned them that all traders among them must have a
license issued by the United States and that they were to
tell him of any British or French or Spanish traders who
were operating without such a license. Then he asked if
they could send a man with him in his boat to inform
other Indian settlements of his mission. He concluded by
making them gifts of tobacco, knives, and whisky.

The address was well received, but the Indians said that
since they were only part of a nation, they could not cede
any lands for the establishment of trading centers.

Actually the Indians had no understanding of land

ownership. All their lands belonged, in their view, to
the whole nation and not to any individual. For a man
to claim a piece of land for himself, thereby depriving
others of the use of it, was in their eyes a far greater crime
than murder. No one was empowered to give a piece of
land to the white men, and this misunderstanding was
at the root of the greater part of the Indian wars that lay
ahead.

Zebulon did not wait for a guide. The Indians said
they would gladly give him one if he could wait a day.
But he was in a hurry to go on and so he left without the
guide. Not very much farther up the river, he found an
excellent site for a fort and trading post, and wrote to
General Wilkinson about it.

All the way up the river, Zebulon hunted his food. Two
men of his company, Corporal Bradley and Private John
Sparks, were good shots, though Zebulon himself was the
best of the group.

Once when Zeb went ashore to hunt with Corporal
Bradley, he took two of his dogs with him. The dogs
became tired from the heat and lay down to rest. He went
on with the corporal, thinking the dogs would follow, but
they had not done so by the time he got back to the river.
Two of the soldiers then volunteered to go ashore and
get the dogs. By evening they had not returned, and Zebulon was greatly worried. They were in a wild area, and
he was afraid that they had been attacked by Indians.
Then he thought that they might have gone ahead of him
up the river, and so he went on. But the men did not turn
up the next day nor the day after.

Eventually Zeb and the others met a Scots trader coming
down the river with four canoes loaded with goods. His
name was James Aird, and he knew the surrounding coun-

try well and also the different tribes. He promised to look out for the two missing soldiers.

Ahead lay more rapids. This time there were no guides to get the keelboat through. The men started poling up through the rapids, but were caught in a whirlpool and the rudder was ripped off the keelboat. They managed to get the boat to a shoal area where the rudder was repaired.

Then the wind came up, piping hard out of the southeast. The water was flowing so swiftly that the men could not pole against it, but Zebulon decided that they might get through the rapids if they used the big sail.

He ordered it hoisted, and hardly had he done so when the wind increased to gale force. The spume from the downward flowing water was hurled back up the river by the fury of the wind. The men looked uncertainly at the lieutenant, for if the boat were holed in the rapids, good swimmers though they all were, they could not hope to survive.

But Pike himself took the tiller, and, in the howling gale, they sailed the keelboat up through the rapids. On the way they found three small boats caught fast on the rocks, but were unable to help the occupants. These boats belonged to the Scotsman, James Aird.

So they went on, day by day inquiring at the Indian villages for the two missing men and leaving stern instructions that if they were found, they were to be cared for and well treated. Eventually the soldiers were brought upriver in a boat by a French trapper, whose name was Blondeau, and two Indians. They had become lost on the prairie and for several days had had nothing to eat but some shellfish they had found on the side of the river.

Zebulon agreed to give the trapper Blondeau passage on his boat as far as Prairie du Chien (The Prairie of the Dogs). He had noted that whenever he went ashore in this country to hunt game, all the Indians fled at the sound of the muskets. He asked Blondeau if he knew the reason for this.

"The Indians are afraid of you Americans," said the trapper. "They say that the Americans are not only very brave, but that they love to fight. One reason you do not see many Indians along the river is that the news that an American boat is coming upstream has gone before you and the Indians have fled."

Zeb also learned that there was a war in progress between the Sioux, whose lands they were now entering, and the Sauteur. At the few Indian villages they came to, they were very well received, however, and the soldiers competed with the Indian warriors in jumping contests. They beat all the villagers and word of the prowess of the American "warriors," who could shoot wild duck on the wing and outjump the best jumpers in the Indian villages, traveled ahead of them.

Thus far the weather had on the whole been good, despite sudden rainstorms and occasional gales. But one day toward the end of August, the wind suddenly backed around to the north, and the thermometer tumbled to a few degrees above freezing.

The expedition had gone little more than five hundred miles on its way. There were a thousand miles yet to go up an unmapped river, whose source was unknown. And ahead lay the terrible winter of the northlands.

CHAPTER SEVEN

The Land of the Sioux

P RAIRIE DU CHIEN, at the meeting of the Wisconsin and Mississippi Rivers, was the trading capital of the Old Northwest—a roaring settlement of hard-drinking trappers and traders and their Indian wives and children. It was a place without law, when men settled their differences with muskets or knives, and the miserable saloons, selling trade rum, were open twenty-four hours a day.

Zeb reached Prairie du Chien early in September, one month after setting out from St. Louis. The river ahead, he knew, was wilder and narrower and full of rapids so he got rid of his keelboat here and obtained in exchange for it two smaller boats which would be easier to take through the turbulent waters ahead. He also hired a half-breed guide, Pierre Rousseau, who knew the language of the Sioux, into whose country they were now headed.

Two days' travel above Prairie du Chien he made con-

tact with the first chief of the Sioux nation—Chief Wabasha. The meeting was startling. The party came to
the chief's village on the banks of the river, and as they
eased their boats over toward it, a band of warriors assembled and fired a ragged volley, the bullets whistling
around the boats and plummeting into the water on all
sides.

"It is only a salute of welcome," Rousseau the guide
explained hastily to Zeb.

"Someone ought to tell them not to load with ball when
firing a salute," said Zeb.

To impress the Sioux, he had his men fire three blank
rounds, and then, arming himself with a sword and two
pistols, he went ashore. Chief Wabasha, the head of this
tribe of Sioux, delighted with the noise of the guns and
impressed that Zeb's soldiers had not flinched when the
musket balls came whistling around them, insisted that
Zeb come immediately to his lodge.

Zebulon first of all posted some of his men on guard
around the boats, and took two or three others with him
to the chief's lodge. The men wanted to bring their muskets with them.

"Leave them in the boats," ordered Zeb. "Let them see
that we are not afraid and that we come in friendship."

There was, in fact, nothing to fear, for Chief Wabasha
feasted Zeb with wild rice and venison and then organized
a medicine dance for him. Gaily dressed men and women
took part in this dance, each holding a piece of animal
skin. They would mill around and then stand before
someone in the audience and, pointing the skin at him,
would blow a puff of air out of their mouths.

"They blow something into your body," said Rousseau.
"See." One of the Indians at whom a dancer had puffed
in this manner fell groaning to the ground, where he lay

writhing for some time. Then he got up and joined the dancers. The half-breed guide said that it was a great honor to be shown this medicine dance of the Sioux.

When he left, Zebulon gave the chief a present of tobacco and calico and some liquor. The chief shook his hand in the presence of his warriors, and then the Sioux warriors demanded the right to shake the hands of the American soldiers. The grinning soldiers went through the performance. Then they all got into the boats and pushed off.

They were now pushing into a country of war into which few whites other than traders had ever penetrated. The Sioux, for all their friendliness, were in constant warfare with the Sauteurs and going up river they met a Sioux war party returning from a raid. Rousseau hailed them and asked how many scalps they had lifted.

"None," replied the warriors.

"You are not men but women," shouted Rousseau, his Indian heritage getting the better of him.

At another place they came to some hastily erected earthworks on the prairie. Rousseau explained that when the Sioux were attacked on the prairies, they quickly dug these holes and put their women and children into them. Again Zeb's party saw a band of Sioux warriors in war paint setting out on a raid. Zebulon tried to get them to settle their differences in peace, but he could do nothing to stop them, and the party went on its way.

The weather was now breaking up. Tempestuous rains, driven by booming winds, lashed the gaunt prairies. Crossing a lake in their boats, such a wild storm arose that they were nearly swamped. Jagged streaks of lightning writhed out of the purple sky, illuminating the land for miles around. Thunder reverberated back and forth among the low hills. The two boats got under the lee of an island to weather out the storm, the boats half swamped, and then they pushed on.

Now the flow of the Mississippi was much faster, and the river took on strange colors. At one place the water in the shallow areas was as red as blood. Over the deeps it was as black as ink. A brooding sense of doom seemed to fill the whole landscape. Sometimes the men had to haul the boats upstream all day in the swift current, for sails and poles were useless. They struggled in the near-freezing river with the towropes, soaking wet for days at a time and so tired at the end of each day that they could not eat anything, but fell asleep as soon as they lay down.

Late in September, camped on an island in the river—now called Pike Island—Zebulon got word that several bands of the Sioux were anxious to meet him for a council. There were seven chiefs all told, and the council was held in a tent made of the sails of the boats on the sandy beach of the island. It was the most important council of the whole voyage, for when it was done, Zebulon had obtained from the Sioux a hundred thousand acres of land on each side of the river at this point, on which to construct a military cantonment. On this site was later built Fort St. Anthony which became Fort Snelling, an important military post. Army officers who inspected the site agreed that it was the finest on the Mississippi for the location of a fort.

There was some difficulty over the signing of the treaty, however. When it had been committed to writing, Zebulon asked the chiefs to make their marks at the bottom of the treaty and they were immediately offended.

"We have given our word," they said. "You do not need more than that unless you doubt our honor."

"This is a treaty between you and your Great White Father, who is not here," replied Zebulon. "It is not your word that he would doubt and if he were here himself, no signatures would be required. But he might doubt me, and so that he can be assured that I am not promising something that you have not agreed to, I ask you to sign this treaty."

At this the chieftains signed and received presents of two hundred dollars' worth of trade goods. The site thus obtained included most of the present areas of the twin cities of St. Paul and Minneapolis. The bargain was a great one and the treaty, unlike many others, was never contested.

When the chieftains had left after the council, Zebulon discovered that one of his flags was missing. He did not know whether it had been stolen or lost through the carelessness of one of his soldiers.

The loss of the flag was a grave matter, because the Indians knew the veneration in which the white men held their flags. They fought to the death to prevent their capture and Zebulon knew that he could not allow the flag to remain missing without losing the respect of the Sioux with whom he had just concluded his treaty.

He sent for the soldier who had the job of raising and lowering the flag and guarding it and questioned him closely. The man was evasive in his answers. He did not know what had happened to the emblem, and whether it had been lost or stolen, the man had failed in his duty. Zebulon disciplined him severely, pointing out that the first duty of a soldier was to guard the flag of his country which he had sworn to protect.

Then he sent for one of the Indian chiefs, and said that the loss of the flag was a very serious matter, so serious that he had chastized his own warrior who was responsible for it and had sent a search party down the river to look

for it. Without accusing the chief he asked for his help
in finding the flag.

The next day the principal chief of the Sioux, Little
Crow, came over to the island in his bark canoe. He was
very much perturbed.

"I thought you had all been killed," he said, much relieved to find Zebulon and his men alive.

"Your flag has been found. It was floating in the river,
and when we found it, we thought you had been massacred
for we know that you will not part with your flag unless
you have been killed."

Then he related the story of the finding of the flag.

Another chief of the Sioux had appeared in Little
Crow's village, heavily mutilated and followed by a band
of warriors. His lip had been cut off by one of Little
Crow's warriors.

"Look in my face and you will see what will happen
to your own," the chieftain cried. Little Crow immediately gathered his warriors together, and a battle between
the two bands was about to begin when around a bend
of the river came the flag, floating on the surface of the
water.

Little Crow was astonished by the sight of it.

"That flag," he shouted, "is sacred to the Americans
who are our friends sent to us by the Great White Father.
It has been taken from them by violence for they would
not part with it otherwise. Therefore let us put our own
war aside and go to revenge our white brothers." The
others agreed, and Little Crow immediately set out for
Zebulon's camp.

Zebulon thanked him and gave him presents, and Little
Crow agreed to settle the differences between the two
tribes peacefully.

The way up river now became more and more difficult. Immediately ahead were the falls of St. Anthony. There was a series of rapids at the foot of them and then the falls over which the water thundered, sending up a perpetual cloud of spray in which there were a number of rainbows caused by the reflection of the sunlight. Zebulon had traded one of his heavier boats for a light barge which could be carried by eight men, and thus they were able to pass the rapids.

Once through the rapids, the barge, the other boat, and all the stores had to be taken by land around the falls. Above the falls the river looked smooth, but the calm soon turned into ripples and then to rapids.

In some of these rapids there were deep pools, while at other places there was but a foot of water over the rocks and no passage between them. The men had to get out of the boats and manhandle them up through the rapids, struggling to keep a footing. At times they were up to their knees in water when they were on a ledge of rocks; the next moment the river was foaming around their shoulders.

Sometimes they made only six or seven miles in a day. The stores had been wrapped in deer skins, but the light barge was leaking and the stores were soaked. The men became exhausted and some of them, hoping to avoid the ordeal of struggling hour after hour in the freezing water manhandling the boats, complained of being sick.

Zebulon had no doctor with him, but he knew his men intimately and knew those who were malingering. He cured them by making them walk along the banks in those parts of the river where the boats could be rowed or sailed. Exposed to freezing winds and with heavy loads on their backs to lighten the labor of the men in the boats, they were soon cured of their "sickness." It was harsh treatment, but Zebulon Pike did not spare himself. Of all the men on the expedition, he was the slightest in build. Yet he labored with them in the river and carried loads of a hundred pounds on his back over those places where the boats and their cargoes had to be portaged.

The countryside through which they passed abounded in game. They were now beyond the last civilized settlement and at that part of the river which flows between the present metropolis of Minneapolis and north central Minnesota. To get food for his men, Zebulon had often to spend a day hunting. He shot quail, pheasant, deer, buffalo, and raccoons. He found that it took a hundred and fifty pounds of meat a day to feed the men, and he needed to lay in stores of food for the winter that lay ahead.

One morning in mid-October Zebulon awoke to find that the ground was covered with snow and that it was still falling. Ahead lay a patch of rough water in which the men would have to manhandle the boats. They set off early, and when they came to the rapids, Zebulon jumped overboard into the freezing river, shouting to the men to follow him. Over they went, and for four hours they struggled to get the boats up through the wild water which surged at times over their heads. But it was no use. Two thirds of the way up the rapids, the men's legs and arms were so numbed that they could hardly move. Finally they pulled the boats over to the bank, and Sergeant Kennerman, who was one of the last out of the water, swayed unsteadily on the shore and then fell to the ground, where he vomited a huge quantity of blood. Corporal Bradley was also bleeding internally, and most of the other men were in such poor condition that it was plain they could not go on without many days of rest.

And yet, thought Zebulon, as he sat shivering over a

fire that evening, after tending as best he could to the sick men, to stay here in the open with winter coming on is to die. We must go on.

But what about Sergeant Kennerman and Corporal Bradley and the other men who were too weak to travel? They could not be carried in the boats nor taken in litters over land.

The only thing to do was to build them a fort with a stockade around it and leave them there with sufficient supplies to see them through the winter. For himself, he must push on.

His job was to find the source of the Mississippi. In that he must not fail.

End of an Ordeal

CHAPTER EIGHT

IN THE WILDERNESS, fifteen hundred miles upriver from St. Louis, on the present site of Little Falls, Minnesota, Pike built a fort surrounded by a stockade, in which to leave those of his men who could travel no further. The fort took the better part of two weeks to build. The first American fort erected in this area, it consisted of an outer wall of upright tree trunks thirty-six feet square with a blockhouse on the northwest corner and another on the southwest corner. Zebulon also built two canoes, for he had decided to leave the greater part of his stores and the big boats at the fort and to go from the fort to the source of the river in canoes, carrying only what stores the canoes could hold.

All this work was done with two felling axes for bringing down the trees and three small hatchets. Zeb took a hand in this work himself and also went out with Private

Smart to shoot game to stock the fort and supply himself
for the rest of the journey. Game was plentiful, particularly deer, pheasant, and duck. On some nights he slept
out on the snow-covered prairies, wrapped in a blanket.
Once he awoke to find the grasslands on the opposite bank
of the river afire, and guessed that the fire had been set
by the warlike Sauteurs.

When at last the stockade was finished and the two
canoes launched, Zeb loaded them with supplies. But a
sudden gust of wind hurled out of the bitter prairies,
struck one of the loaded canoes and capsized it. Scores
of cartridges fell into the water and were spoiled. Zeb put
them on blankets and built fires around them, trying to
dry them out. He tried drying out the soaking powder by
breaking the paper cartridges open and heating the
powder in a pot over a fire. The powder blew up, nearly
killing him and a couple of men who were nearby.

The canoes were too small, he decided; so he selected
a big pine and felled it to make a larger one. Meanwhile
the cold increased. Snow, sleet, and wind followed each
other in grim rotation. The river flowed too fast at this
point to freeze. But farther upstream, Zebulon knew, the
water would be freezing fast. His books had all been
packed away, and in the long evenings and nights there
was nothing to do but listen to the moaning of the wind
across the empty prairies and the howl of wolves and the
roaring of the river past the stockade. For the first time
the vast spaces around and their complete solitude began
to oppress him. He could understand now why it was
that men alone in such a wilderness often drank to excess.

The canoe would not be ready for several days, and to
overcome his sense of depression, Pike determined that
he would go downstream and see whether he could kill
an elk. He had seen the spoor of these huge beasts many

times and had sighted one or two in the distance, but had never shot one. He convinced himself that he needed the meat, but the plain fact was that he knew he must have something to occupy himself with, mentally and physically, while waiting for the canoe to be finished.

Off he went then, taking with him Private Miller, an easygoing man who was a good shot. They found a herd of elk and followed it two days, sleeping in the open at night. Zebulon got a shot at one buck with a spread of ten feet between the horns. He hit it in the shoulder, but his ball was too light and the wounded animal was able to get away. He brought a deer down with a shot between the eyes, but when he went to it, the deer got up and ran off. It was only stunned by the light musket ball. Eventually Zebulon managed to kill an elk, but the men had now been away from camp for several days, and they were almost out of food. He and Miller cut off some of the elk's meat, and while they cooked it over a fire of hemlock boughs, wolves fought over the rest of the carcass a few yards away.

Continuing to hunt, Zebulon shot several deer. But the deer, though wounded, were able to get away, and Zebulon was not sufficiently experienced as a tracker to follow them until they dropped. Eventually he got a store of venison put up and decided, since it was more than the two of them could carry, to leave Miller with the meat while he went back to the fort for help. But he had underestimated the distance they had gone.

While hunting, he had severely twisted his ankle, and his moccasins were worn out. He mended them with a needle made of the bone of the elk and used the animal's sinews for thread as the Indians did. After walking a few hours, his feet and ankles had swollen so much that the elk sinews were cutting into his flesh. He stumbled on in

agony, buffeted by the wind. Finally, unable to bear the
pain any more, he took off the moccasins and went bare-
footed in the snow. It was in this condition that he was
met by a party of his men from the fort.

Pike had learned two important facts about life in the
wilderness. The first was that his musketballs were too
light to bring down big game. If they were to be killed,
it must be through the heart or some equally vital spot.
Secondly, he must get more experience in tracking down
wounded animals.

Still the party was not ready to resume the journey upriver. The men, getting one of the canoes over some rocks
during a hunting expedition, split it open. Pike, in desperation, with winter setting in fast, made some sledges,
deciding that he might well travel overland up the river
or use the sledges on the ice if the river froze. Then the
weather turned mild for a while, the snow on the prairie
melted, and the sledges of course could not travel over the
mud. Several groups of Sioux came to the stockade and
camped around it, delaying his departure further. But at
last Pike set off, leaving Sergeant Kennerman in charge of
the stockade. There were plenty of stores to last him and
also to supply the explorers when they returned.

Before they started out the party divided into two: one
traveling along the bank, pulling the sledges; the other
going by water in the canoes. The men hauling the sledges
had the better task, for although the snow was largely gone
and they had to struggle forward with their huge load
through the mud, those in the canoes had often to get into
the frigid water to guide the canoes through the rapids.

As they proceeded northward, the weather seemed determined to be perverse. A few days out, and the snow
on the prairie had all melted, leaving a thick gluey mud
around hummocks of grass. In this the heavy sledges

stuck so that they could be dragged forward only one at a time. When the men had hauled one heavily laden sledge half a mile, they had to leave it and go back for the other. They had to continue in this back-and-forth fashion, staggering and slipping in the mud, their chests heaving with the exertion, their backs and legs aching. On the river, with the canoes, matters were no better. One series of rapids followed another. Progress was painfully slow. One day the party made seven miles, the next day five, the next day four. Then they had to stop for two days, for the men were too exhausted to go any farther.

All the time there was the problem of hunting game to supply food. Sometimes Zeb walked as much as twenty-five miles hunting game and would find on his return that in his absence the party had been able to advance only three miles. He would return so tired that he could hardly make the necessary notes in his journal. And there were always problems to deal with—a runner broken on a sledge, a barrel of stores split, a man with a lacerated foot. All these matters he must attend to before he could wrap himself in his blanket and sleep.

Finally he decided that they must cache some of the stores and pick them up on their return. A big hole was dug and a barrel of flour and one of salt pork, both wrapped in deerskins, were buried in it. When the hole was covered up, they lit a fire over it so that Indians would assume that it was merely the camping site of a party of Sioux or Chippeways.

On Christmas Day Zebulon and his men made three miles upriver. Zebulon decided to rest the men and to give them each two extra pounds of meat, two extra pounds of flour, and a little whisky and tobacco to celebrate the day. Because of the cold and the heavy work, the men ate enormous quantities of meat. The two extra pounds were welcome.

The next day, struggling from dawn to dark, they again made only three miles. The weather turned suddenly colder, and the river was frozen in many spots. Now the sledges were hauled along the ice with the canoes on top of them. But time and again the ice broke under the weight of the sledges, and the men were plunged into the water where they struggled, hands and legs freezing, trying to haul the sledge out. Toes and fingers became frostbitten.

Rousseau, the half-breed guide, showed Zebulon a kind of tree growing near the river called a sap pine. "The resin in the cones cures frostbite," he said.

At night the men rubbed the resin on their toes, which were turning white from frostbite, and consoled themselves that this was doing them good. They remained cheerful and obedient, squeezing out a laugh when one or the other fell through the ice into the river. Though they were not aware of it, they were becoming tougher than the Indians through whose territory they were passing.

Rousseau was greatly afraid of the tribes in this area. They were for the most part Chippeways and sworn enemies of the Sioux. Once Zeb's party passed the camp of a Chippeway war party and learned that the braves had raided a party of Sioux and killed four men and four women. Further on they came to six beautifully made birch bark canoes by the side of the river. Zebulon had made it a daily practice to go ahead of the men to explore the country and hunt. Rousseau now begged him not to do so, as he would be mistaken by the Chippeway for a Sioux trader and shot.

"I don't think they would kill two lone men," said

Zebulon. "In any case, someone has to do the hunting and exploring."

A few days later, around dusk, a large party of Indians came whooping down on their camp by the river.

"Stand by your guns," Zebulon ordered.

But the alert was unnecessary. The Indians were indeed Chippeways, but they were led by an English trader, Cuthbert Grant, who was the agent of the Northwest Fur Company in this wilderness. The whole area was now American, but the Indians did not know this, and in any case it would have made little difference to them.

The Englishman, Grant, took Zebulon to his trading headquarters, and Zebulon was angered to find that over the post the Union Jack of Great Britain was flying. "You're flying the wrong flag there, Mr. Grant," he said sharply.

"Oh, that's not my flag at all," Grant said hurriedly. "It belongs to the Indians. I know that this is American territory now."

The explanation did little to mollify Pike, who found that the Northwest Fur Trading Company was taking huge profits out of the area which might be American in name, but was in British hands as far as commerce was concerned. He called a council of the Indians and told them they were now subjects of the Great White Father in Washington. The Indians were amazed that an American party should have come so far north. They knew of the Americans only by reputation and believed them the fiercest of all the white "tribes." Indeed they paid the Americans the compliment of calling them "white Indians."

Pike was now far into northern Minnesota and near the Canadian border. The Mississippi flowed through a land abounding in lakes, some a few miles long, others of much greater size. Cedar Lake, Sandy Lake, Lake Win-

nibigoshish, Cass Lake, and Lake Bemidji—these are some
of the lakes in this northern waterland through which the
great river flows. Pike visited most of these lakes, though
three feet of snow had fallen and the going was exception-
ally hard. He pushed on ahead of his party many times,
spending nights in the wilderness with an Indian guide
with whom he could communicate only by sign language.

By the first week in January all the men in his party had
frozen fingers or noses or toes. The cold was beyond anything Zebulon had ever experienced. Chillblain made the
men's hands a mass of bloody plum-colored flesh. They
could advance only by three-mile stages. Zebulon would
go ahead and light a fire three miles ahead of the party
so they could warm themselves when they reached it. But
finally the day came when the men could travel no farther.

Zebulon left them in camp and pushed on ahead with
Corporal Miller, searching for the source of the great
river which was now reduced to little more than a stream.
His own legs were swollen so badly from exposure that he
could not put on his clothes. His feet and ankles were
twice their normal size. He had had to borrow clothing
big enough to cover his swollen legs, from a trader of the
Northwest Fur Company. It was half an hour's work to
stand up in the morning, and the blood ran like fire
through his enlarged legs when he got out of bed.

"You're a fool to walk around like this," the trader
said. "Rest a while until your legs are better."

Zebulon shook his head. He must find the source of the
river and then get his men back out of the frozen north-
land. So he pushed on. The Indians had said that the
river rose in a small lake—Leech Lake—not many miles
away. The way led through frozen swamps and morasses
of reeds and grasses which grew higher than a man.

Zebulon skirted several small lakes and crossed a number of tributaries flowing into the Mississippi.

On February 1, 1806, coming through a grove of maples that grew by the river, he came at last to a small lake. The surface was frozen and on the far side he could see a trading post of the Northwest Fur Company.

This was Leech Lake, the source of the Mississippi River, as he had been told. His journey was at an end. He squatted silently on his swollen legs on the ice of the lake, staring across its gray surface.

"Tired, sir?" asked Corporal Miller.

"No," said Zebulon, "but this is the end of our journey, Corporal. It's time to head back to St. Louis."

"You mean this is what we came all the way to find?" asked Miller.

"Yes," said Zebulon.

"Well," said the stolid Corporal, "I can't say that I think very much of it."

Before starting on the long journey south to St. Louis, Pike called a meeting of the principal chiefs of the Chippeway in the region. He told them what he had told all the other Indians at such council meetings—that they were now the children of the Great White Father in Washington, that they must give up the medals and flags they had received from the British, and that they must live in peace with one another. Zebulon had been ordered to bring some of the Indians of the warring tribes back to St. Louis so that their differences could be resolved. He therefore asked the chieftains to select delegates to be sent with him to St. Louis so that peace between the Chippeway and the Sioux could be arranged.

But the chiefs were unwilling to do this. The journey

was long and through hostile territory, and they needed their young warriors with them in case of attack.

"Are there no men among you brave enough to make this journey and carry the peace pipe to St. Louis?" demanded Zebulon. "Am I talking to soldiers or to women at this council meeting?" The jibe went home and soon forty or fifty warriors offered to make the journey with him to St. Louis. He selected two, whom he adopted in the presence of the Council of chiefs as his children.

There was one more duty he had to perform—a very important duty. On the northern shore of Leech Lake there was, as noted, a trading post of the Northwest Fur Company. Its proprietor was Hugh McGillis, and over the fort was flying the British flag.

McGillis was very hospitable to Pike, giving him supplies, clothing, and sledges. But Zebulon was determined that McGillis as well as the Chippeway Indians should know that this was now American territory.

He therefore wrote a formal letter to McGillis forbidding him to fly the British flag over his post, to distribute British flags or medals to the Indians (the usual method of obtaining their loyalty), or to sell them liquor. He also notified him that he must get a license from the United States Government to continue trading, and that he must pay the proper duty to the United States Government on all British goods imported from Canada.

McGillis readily agreed to all these terms, put his agreement in writing, and offered to take down the Union Jack. But Zebulon decided on a ceremony to impress on the Indians that this was now American territory.

Accordingly he got together a number of his men and some of the Indians and ordered them to shoot the Union Jack down from on top of the fort. The Indians hesitated, looking at McGillis.

"Go ahead," said Zebulon. "He is not in authority. I am. And I order the flag shot down."

The soldiers fired first, and then the Indians joined in. The Union Jack fluttered to the ground, and Zebulon then raised the Stars and Stripes in its stead. He suspected that when he was gone, the Union Jack would be raised again, but he had given the Chippeways a demonstration of who was the real power in the land and had shaken their loyalty to Britain.

A few days later he gave the order to march south. Zebulon decided to travel across country in dogsleds rather than down the river, there being several feet of snow on the ground. His legs and ankles were still swollen, and his physical condition worse than that of the soldiers with him. He would not ride on one of the sleds because of the roughness of the ground, but walked beside them on snowshoes, which were called in those days rackets. The strings of the snowshoes cut into his swollen feet through his thin moccasins, and his feet bled constantly. He was able to walk only slowly across the rough areas, but soon they were in good territory and he was able to ride a sled. No longer hauling boats in freezing water up the turbulent river, the explorers were able to make fast progress, covering in one day a distance that had taken them three days going upriver.

Soon Zebulon was back at the fort he had constructed and left in the charge of Sergeant Kennerman. Here he learned that the sergeant had flagrantly disobeyed his orders during his absence. He had sold several smoked hams of venison that Zebulon had prepared to take back to his commanding officer, General Wilkinson. He had squandered the flour and pork and liquor with which the fort had been stocked, and had even broken into Zebulon's chest and sold several of his personal possessions to the Indians.

Zebulon held an inquiry into the sergeant's conduct, found him guilty, and broke him to a private. The punishment was lenient, but Zebulon remembered the unfailing cheerfulness of the man on the journey upriver, his willingness to jump into the freezing river to heave the boats through the rapids when needed, and the fact that this giant of a man had worked so hard on one occasion that blood had poured from his mouth.

He was a good soldier then, but authority went to his head. So Zebulon decided that demotion was sufficient punishment.

At the fort there were more conferences with the local chiefs, designed to promote peace among them. The two warriors of the Chippeways who were to come to St. Louis had deserted the party farther north, and Zebulon had neither the time nor the men to go after them. He believed, however, that the Indians were sincere when they pledged peace in the future. Certainly they had treated him well, providing him with food and shelter when needed and staging tribal dances for him. One chieftain related how, during the Revolutionary War, the British had tried to persuade him to attack the Americans. The chieftain had refused to take sides.

"You are all the same people to us," he had told the British officer. "Now you quarrel among yourselves, and who am I to decide which side is right and which side is wrong? It is a white man's war, and I will keep my warriors for the wars among the redmen."

At another village they met a young squaw whose skin was very light. It was explained that her father was an American trader and that he had deserted the mother and the girl.

"Well, then, you're a countryman of mine," said Zeb and he gave the squaw a little gift. This the Indians found very amusing, and thereafter the young squaw was called the Bostonian.

It was April, however, before the ice on the river had broken up sufficiently for Zeb to load his boats and begin the long downriver journey to St. Louis. Even so, he stopped several times on the way to confer with the chiefs and traders he had met when coming up the Mississippi. He found that the solemn pledges of peace among the tribes were not being kept. The chieftains might pledge the peace, but the warriors would have no part of it. Their standing in the tribe depended on their bravery in battle, and warfare was a sport among them. It was disheartening, but peace was not to be brought to tribes who had been at war for hundreds of years by the visit of a young lieutenant and a handful of soldiers. Still, Zebulon believed that the very fact that a small detachment of soldiers had penetrated clean through the Indian country, visiting one tribe after another, could not fail to impress on the Indians the determination of the United States to bring order to their lands.

The rest of the journey downstream was without incident. Traveling south, Pike was soon out of the dreadful northern winter, and he was back in St. Louis on April 30, 1806, after an absence of eight months and twenty-two days.

CHAPTER NINE

New Assignment

CHAPTER NINE

*Z*EBULON PIKE had accomplished a huge task, though for many years historians were inclined to belittle the results. It was claimed for instance that he had not found the true source of the Mississippi for the source has since been found to be at Lake Itasca, twenty-six miles from Lake Leech. But Pike had got within twenty-six miles of the true source of the mighty river. With his legs so swollen that he could not get into his own clothing, it seemed hardly necessary to go those last few miles, especially when the great river in its headwaters was split into a number of streams, any one of which could be claimed to be the Mississippi and the others merely tributaries.

He had negotiated for sites for forts and trading posts which would be of the greatest importance in the development of the country in later years. He had mapped the course of the river with remarkable accuracy, consider-

93

ing the primitive instruments he had to use. He had charted the shoals, provided copious notes on the width of the river and speed of the current at different points, on the abundance of game in the areas along its banks, on the amount and kinds of timber to be found, and so on.

He had visited the chieftains of a dozen tribes, acquainting them with the fact that they were now under the care of the United States government. He had impressed on the pro-British traders of the Mississippi wilderness that they were now subject to the law of the United States. And perhaps most important of all, he had, having explored the Louisiana Purchase lands to their northernmost limit along the Mississippi and displayed the American flag, giving his country a firm claim to disputed territory. The area which was to become the state of Minnesota was a sort of no-man's-land between Canada and the United States, and both claimed jurisdiction over it. But Pike's bold penetration of it and his shooting down of the British flag over the trading post on Lake Leech gave the United States a clear claim to the territory which was later ceded without great argument by the British.

President Jefferson, who was kept in touch with Pike's expedition by General Wilkinson, was so pleased with the results that in a message to Congress on December 2, 1806, he praised Pike, saying "Very useful additions have been made to our knowledge of the Mississippi by Lieutenant Pike, who has ascended to its source and whose journal will be made ready for communication to both Houses of Congress."

Zebulon Pike, however, was not to have much time in which to recuperate from his adventures and write a full account of his exploration for the Congress. He was hardly back in St. Louis, reunited with his wife and daughter, before General Wilkinson had another task for him.

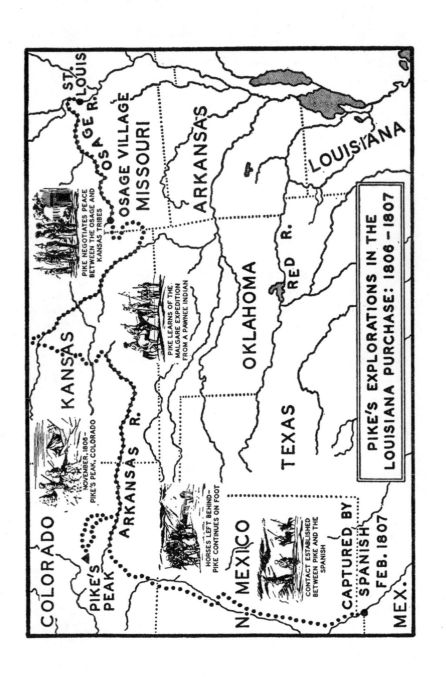

ST. LOUIS

OSAGE R.

OSAGE VILLAGE

MISSOURI

ARKANSAS

LOUISIANA

PIKE NEGOTIATES PEACE
BETWEEN THE OSAGE AND
KANSAS TRIBES

PIKE LEARNS OF THE
MALGARE EXPEDITION
FROM A PAWNEE INDIAN

RED R.

OKLAHOMA

KANSAS

NOVEMBER, 1806—
PIKE'S PEAK, COLORADO

ARKANSAS R.

TEXAS

COLORADO

PIKE'S
PEAK

HORSES LEFT BEHIND—
PIKE CONTINUES ON FOOT

N. MEXICO

CONTACT ESTABLISHED
BETWEEN PIKE AND THE
SPANISH

CAPTURED BY
SPANISH
FEB. 1807

MEX.

PIKE'S EXPLORATIONS IN THE
LOUISIANA PURCHASE: 1806–1807

The General now ordered Pike on an expedition to explore the southwestern part of the Louisiana Purchase. Again he was to venture into a no-man's-land, over which both the United States and Spain claimed jurisdiction. It would be many years before the boundaries between the territory of the United States and of Spain would be exactly fixed in this area.

Because he was likely to come upon Spanish parties in the area, Wilkinson warned Pike to be careful to avoid conflict with them. He would, he was told, be held personally responsible for any clash with the Spaniards. The two countries were almost on the verge of war over the boundary question, and Zebulon was to be careful not to provoke a conflict.

Pike's orders on this expedition fell into several parts. He was first of all to restore about fifty captured Osage warriors, their wives and children, to their homes on the Grand Osage River and to establish peace between the Osage Indians and their traditional enemies, the Kansas tribe. He was then to penetrate into the territory of the Pawnees and the Comanches to the west and establish good relations with them. He would explore the Osage, a tributary of the Missouri, to its source, and then head south to the Arkansas River. At this point part of his group would return down the Arkansas to the Mississippi. He himself, would go upstream to establish the source of the Arkansas River and then, striking south again, pick up the Red River and descend this to the Mississippi. He was to start immediately.

Pike was never a man to dally once he got his orders. He had returned to St. Louis the last day of April, 1806. But July fifteenth he was off again on his new exploration. Eighteen of the soldiers who had accompanied him to the source of the Mississippi volunteered for the western expedition, among them Kennerman, now reduced from sergeant to private, and Private John Sparks. Pike also had with him Lieutenant James B. Wilkinson, son of General Wilkinson, and Dr. John H. Robinson, who volunteered to accompany them as a surgeon. The party traveled in two keelboats, one being needed for the Indians.

Both keelboats had big masts and sails, but in the flat, dead heat of the summer, hardly a breath of air stirred, and Zebulon soon dumped the sails and masts as just so much dead weight.

The men rowed the huge boats with the sweeps or, where the water was shallow enough, poled them along. Several men would take one end of a sweep and putting the other on the river bottom walk pushing against it from the bow of the keelboat to the stern, thus heaving the huge vessel foot by foot up the river. Where the current was too swift for poling, but the river was not deep, the men got out and manhandled the boats forward. Sometimes there were parties of men in the water pushing the boats and others on land hauling them with towropes. These were the same men who had jumped willingly into the icy waters of the Mississippi in midwinter to undertake the same work. But it was pleasant for them now in the hot sun to get into the cool, crystal-clear water. The Indians traveled along the land to lighten the boats, though their women and children stayed aboard.

The Indians camped apart from the whites at night and awakened everybody at dawn with their howling, for it was their custom at dawn each day to bemoan their dead and ask the Great Spirit to preserve their lives until they were able to obtain revenge for relatives who had been killed by their enemies.

They were not long started on their journey before Private Kennerman deserted. He complained of not feeling well and was allowed to join the land party following the boats by the side of the river. Then he disappeared and no trace of him was ever found. He had been brooding over his reduction from sergeant to private and had decided that the army was no place for him.

The countryside through which they were passing was very beautiful and full of game. Zeb was able to supply all the meat that his huge party needed, shooting deer, buffalos, turkeys, and geese. In addition the men caught a number of fish in the river. One day while out hunting, Zeb very nearly stepped on a huge rattlesnake. The snake drew itself in and so his foot missed landing on it. Dr. Robinson was following close behind and almost stepped on the snake too, but managed to jump aside. Zebulon, curious about the snake, poked it with his ramrod.

"Watch out," cried Dr. Robinson. "It will strike and kill you."

"It could have killed me a minute before and didn't. Why should it do so now?" asked Zeb.

The snake writhed under the probing of the ramrod, but made no move to strike. Dr. Robinson said Zeb should kill it.

"No," he replied. "It spared my life. Why should I be so ungrateful as to kill it in return? A man must surely be at least as generous as a snake."

Dr. Robinson wondered just what kind of a man this Lieutenant Zebulon Pike was. He had heard that Pike was perhaps the sternest disciplinarian in the army on the western frontier. Yet he spared the life of a rattlesnake which had not struck at him. He was a strange man indeed.

A little later, Dr. Robinson saw another side of Zeb's character—the stern unbending side that would permit no compromise when a matter of principle was involved. One of the soldiers complained that his coonskin cap had been stolen by one of the Osage chiefs. The cap had the soldier's initials on it and he could prove that it was his property.

The party was deep in Indian territory by this time, and the Indian captives were not very friendly and quarreled often among themselves. Perhaps the best thing to do would be to ignore the theft of the soldier's cap so as not to offend the Osage warriors.

But that was not Zebulon Pike's way. He called the Osage chief who had the soldier's cap and told him to return it. "I don't say you stole it because I have no proof that you did," Zebulon said. "Nonetheless, you have it, and it is not your property. See that it is returned to the man or it will be the worse for you."

The chief immediately returned the cap to the soldier, and the word went around among the Indians that Zebulon Pike was not a man to be trifled with. Up to that time, there had been a considerable amount of petty thieving of the soldiers' property. Now it stopped.

It was not long before the party reached the village where the prisoners were to be returned to their people. The wives of the returned warriors threw themselves into the arms of their husbands, children hugged their returned fathers with tears streaming down their faces. One of the chiefs of the village made a speech in which he said:

"Osage! You now see your wives, our brothers, your daughters, your sons redeemed from captivity. Who did this? Was it the Spaniards? No. The French? No. Had either of these people been governors of the country, your relatives might have rotted in captivity, and you would never have seen them again. But the Americans stretched forth their hands and they are restored to you. What can you do in return for this goodness? Nothing. All your lives would not suffice to repay their bounty."

The return of the prisoners established the best relations between the United States and the Osage nation, at least for the time being. Zebulon spent several weeks with the Osages, conferring with their chiefs, who were very hospitable. He found the Osages divided their menfolk into three classes—warriors and hunters, cooks, and medicine men. The cooks were often old hunters who could no longer go out after game. One of the chiefs summoned his medicine men to impress Zebulon and his party with their magic. They put on a surprising show. Some thrust huge knives down their throats, allowing the blood from the wounds to well from their mouths. Others swallowed bones and pretended to produce them again from their nostrils. One medicine man asked Zebulon what reward he would receive if he put a stick through his tongue, cut off the end of his tongue, and then put the severed tip in place again.

"I'll give you a deerskin shirt," said Zebulon.

The medicine man stood before him and, appearing to be in great pain, seemed to force a pointed stick through his tongue. Then a warrior was invited to cut the end of the tongue off, which he did and held it up for everyone to see. A second later the medicine man had taken it, put it in his mouth, withdrawn the stick, and shown his tongue whole again.

But Zebulon was not deceived. He knew that the medicine man could not possibly have had his tongue cut in two in this manner, but was only pretending, and that what he held up for everyone to see was not the end of his tongue but a piece of meat.

"I'll make you another bargain," said Zebulon. "Do that again but let *me* cut off the end of your tongue. If you can put it in place again, I will give you twenty deer-skin shirts."

But the medicine man refused this offer.

The Osages were so friendly that they were an embarrassment to Zebulon. In one day he had to partake of as many as a dozen meals in the lodges of different chiefs. The food was always the same, corn boiled in buffalo fat with at times a little meat. It was eaten with the hands out of a common pot. But one chief set a plate, knife, and fork before Zeb, explaining proudly that he had been back in the white man's territory on a visit and had observed that this was the way white men liked to eat.

Zebulon arranged several meetings with chiefs of the Osage and the Kansas tribes. These two tribes were enemies, but he negotiated a solemn peace between them, and when at last he was able to set out for the Arkansas River, several braves and warriors of the Osage and Kansas tribes went with him. He wanted now to arrange peace between these two tribes and the Pawnees who were reckoned the most warlike tribe in the area.

Zebulon had been delayed longer than he had planned among the Osages, and it was mid-September before he got into Pawnee territory. Here the character of the land changed. The lush grasslands to the north now gave way to rolling expanses of sandy waste on which only a thin grass grew. Game was still plentiful. There were so many deer, elk, buffalos, and antelopes about that one man with a rifle could shoot enough game to feed two hundred men a day. Wild animals could live on the thin grasses of this area, which later became known as the Great American Desert, but Zebulon did not believe that the area could be settled, for the land was not good for farming.

One day, riding with his mixed party of Indian chiefs and United States soldiers, Zeb saw a lone horseman galloping over the sand dunes ahead toward him. The Osage and Kansas chiefs with him looked uneasily at the rider, who was naked except for a loin cloth. He carried a bow and arrow and a spear and rode magnificently without benefit of a saddle.

"Pawnee," said one of the Osage chiefs to Zebulon.

Few Americans had ever met a member of the Pawnee nation before. They were magnificent horsemen and great hunters and fighters. The Pawnee reined his horse in out of bow shot of Zeb's party and held up his hand as a sign that he came in peace.

"You are not Spaniards?" the Pawnee asked, looking over Zebulon's group.

"No," said Zebulon, speaking through an interpreter. "We are American warriors sent by the Great White Father in Washington. Why do you ask if we are Spanish?"

"Many Spaniards passed this way a few days ago," said the Pawnee. "They rode beautiful white horses and had plenty of guns and much ammunition."

Spaniards? So deep in American territory? Could it be that the United States and Spain were at war? What other reason could there be for a company of Spanish cavalry to have come so deeply into the territory of the United States?

Zebulon questioned the Pawnee hunter further. He learned that there were about six hundred of the Spanish and that they had visited most of the Pawnee villages. They had rounded up many white traders and taken them back to Sante Fe and had forced others to travel east, back to the Mississippi.

When he got to the Pawnee village, Zebulon learned further details of this mysterious Spanish party from Chief White Wold. It had been headed by a Lieutenant Mal-

gares, and one of its objects had been, it seemed, to inter-
cept Zebulon himself and prevent his traveling farther
west. News of his expedition, then, had already reached
the Spanish. Another object was to impress on the Indians
that Spain was the greatest power and that they had better
side with the Spanish against the Americans.

When he learned of this attempt by the Spanish to win
over the Indians in American territory by a show of force,
Zebulon called a council of the Pawnees, at which four
hundred warriors were present, as were the chiefs of the
Kansas and Osage nations who had accompanied him.

The Spaniards, he found, had left several Spanish flags
with the Pawnee chiefs and had issued many medals to
them to retain their loyalty. A Spanish flag, he noted,
flew before the door of the council house in which the
meeting was held, although it was deep in American
territory. What the British were doing in the northern
part of the Louisiana Purchase the Spanish were doing
in the southwestern part, and he must put a stop to it.

Zebulon lost no time in telling the Pawnees that they
were now under the protection of the United States. They
must give up the Spanish medals which they had been
given and also the Spanish flags. They would get American
medals and American flags. Although he had but twenty
men with him, he was determined to have the Pawnees
acknowledge American sovereignty.

The chiefs and warriors grumbled among themselves.
They did not want to part with the Spanish flags or medals.
The Spanish party that had visited them only a few weeks
before had numbered six hundred men. All were mounted
on beautiful white horses, except their leaders, who rode
coal-black stallions. Plainly Spain was more powerful
than America. Zebulon Pike's little band of twenty rag-

ged soldiers could not compare with the show the Spaniards had put on.

But Zebulon was not to be put off. Standing up in the council house, surrounded by hostile warriors who outnumbered him twenty to one, he repeated his demands.

"The Pawnee nations cannot have two fathers," he cried. "They must either be the children of the Spanish or acknowledge their American father. The Spanish flag outside this council house must be brought to me, for this is American territory. In return I will give you an American flag which must be flown in its stead."

When he had finished speaking, nobody said a word. Zebulon knew that he could not enforce his demand. He was trying to bluff, ordering the Pawnees to take down the Spanish flag and bring it to him. If they refused, he might not get out of the council house alive. Still no one spoke, and the silence was almost more than Pike could bear. Then one of the oldest of the chiefs rose and without a word went to the door of the council house. All watched him. He returned with the Spanish flag which he laid at Zebulon's feet.

Zebulon smiled at the old chief. "You have done well," he said. He unrolled the Stars and Stripes and gave the flag to the chief. "Raise this on the flagpole outside the council house," he said.

The Osage and Kansa warriors who were present at this council were plainly relieved. They had accepted their American standing, but were fearful that the Pawnees would not. That would mean warfare between them. But the Pawnees, even after the Stars and Stripes had been raised outside their lodge, looked grave. Zebulon knew what was troubling them. What would happen to them if, when he had gone, the big Spanish force came back and found the Pawnees flying the American flag? They would be massacred. Of that there could be little doubt. And there would be no American troops to defend them.

Realizing their plight, Zeb now made a gesture that won him the friendship of the Pawnees—at least for the time being.

"You have shown yourselves dutiful children in acknowledging your American father," he said. "The Americans desire only that their red brothers live in peace around their own campfires and do not get embroiled in the wars between the white nations. Therefore I am going to return to you the Spanish flag, in case the Spaniards should return to this village after I have gone. But this flag is not to be raised in the village while I and my men are here. You are to use it only to protect yourselves from the Spaniards, should they return."

There was a shout of relief from the Pawnees, and resentment against Zebulon and his men was replaced by friendship. During his stay only the Stars and Stripes was displayed by the Pawnee chiefs.

Immediately after this meeting, Zebulon wrote a full report to Secretary of War Henry Dearborn and General Wilkinson about the invasion of American territory by Spanish troops.

The meeting had taken place in a huge council lodge of the Pawnees. Its walls were of earth supported on the inside by a network of stakes driven into the ground. The roof was dome-shaped and over eleven feet high at the center. There was an entrance tunnel, also of earth, and Zebulon discovered that the Pawnees were on the verge of developing a civilization of their own. Their houses were not unlike those that had once been built in England, and in Europe generally, seven hundred years before. The nation was turning to farming and not only bred horses, but also raised corn, beans, and squash and other vegetables. They had learned how to irrigate their fields in a primitive manner. Furthermore, their towns were fortified with a palisade of stakes driven into the ground surrounding them. The Pawnees were among the most advanced of the Indian tribes he had met.

Visiting one "town" a day after the council meeting, Zeb got more details of the Spanish expedition which had passed by only a few weeks previously. The chief told him that the Spaniards had come to conclude treaties with all the tribes in that area. They had intended to push even farther eastward, well into American territory, to make pacts with the Kansas and Osages and other tribes.

"I persuaded them not to travel farther east, but to turn back, as they had come far enough," said the chief. "And now I say that you have come far enough and should turn back also."

"My orders are to go farther west, to the land of the Comanches," replied Zeb. "And I am to trace the Arkansas River to its source."

"You must go back," the chief insisted. "I told the Spaniards that I would not let you go farther."

"I will go on," said Zebulon quietly. "Those are my orders."

"Then," said the chieftain, "I will stop you with my warriors. You are only a few, and we number hundreds."

"You will have to learn something about the Americans," said Zebulon. "We will not be turned back by threats. If you kill us, there will be others who will come after us. If you kill them, there will be more, and your whole nation will suffer."

On that they parted.

When he left the Osage River to head across country to the Arkansas, Pike had sold his boats and obtained some horses from the Osage tribes. They were poor beasts, however, and he got better animals among the Pawnees. He now set out again for the Arkansas River where Lieutenant Wilkinson would go downstream while he went up to the headwaters.

The morning of his departure, however, he discovered that two of his horses had been stolen. The Pawnees had turned hostile, following Zebulon's interview with the chief who wanted the Americans to go no farther west. Zebulon demanded the return of the horses, but got back only one. He started out, making a wide circuit of the Pawnee village in case of attack. He ordered his men, if attacked, to hold their fire until the Pawnees were only five or six paces from them. They were to fire then and immediately charge into the mass of the Pawnees with saber and bayonet.

Having given these orders, he then turned to Lieutenant Wilkinson, his second in command, and said, "I'm going to get back my horse."

Wilkinson shrugged. When Zebulon Pike made up his mind, argument was futile. Taking with him only an interpreter and one soldier, Private Sparks, Zebulon rode boldly into the Pawnee village and reined in in front of the lodge of the chieftain. The village was full of young warriors, armed with bows and arrows, guns, and lances.

The chief came out, and, ignoring the warriors, Zebulon said to him, "Your men have stolen one of my horses. I want it back. I am going to leave this soldier here until noon tomorrow while you find the horse. When you have found it, send my soldier back with it. And remember, this one soldier represents thousands. See that no harm comes to him. The Spanish may have to come into your country with six hundred men. But we Americans need only twenty for the same work." Then he turned and rode slowly out of the village, leaving Private Sparks alone with hundreds of warlike Pawnees.

Again, as in the council house, Zebulon's bluff paid off. The next morning Private Sparks caught up with him. He was grinning from ear to ear and leading the stolen horse.

"Any trouble?" asked Zebulon.

"No, sir," said Sparks. "No trouble. But I felt pretty lonesome back there among all those savages."

"When you were alone in the Pawnee village," said Zebulon, "you represented the Great White Father—the President of the United States. And," he added with a rare twinkle, "that doesn't often happen to a private soldier."

"No, sir," said Sparks, "and if you don't mind my saying so, sir, once in a lifetime is often enough."

Zebulon laughed. Later Lieutenant Wilkinson asked him if he thought it worthwhile to risk the life of a soldier for a horse.

"If I had not got that horse back," said Zebulon, "I would have been risking the lives of the whole party. The Pawnees could easily steal every horse we have. They could attack and slaughter us all. By leaving Sparks to get the horse, I have shown them that we trust them, are not afraid of them, and are to be respected. When you have only a few men, you must put on a bold face or all is lost. We have achieved as much respect from the Pawnees with twenty men as the Spaniards got with six hundred. That is something worth thinking about."

CHAPTER TEN

Mountain of Destiny

CHAPTER TEN

STRIKING SOUTH toward the Arkansas River, Zebulon Pike was leading the first American party ever to explore the great plains of the Middle West. He was pioneering the way for the huge westward migration of Americans into this unknown area.

He found himself, as he approached the Arkansas, in what he described as a paradise on earth—vast rolling grasslands that swept magnificently westward to the horizon, numerous rivers and streams, whose waters were crystal clear, and all about a huge quantity of game—buffalo, deer, elk, and wild mustangs in such multitudes that he could scarcely believe what he saw.

Topping a rise one day, he found the land before him one moving ocean of buffalo, pressing slowly forward, their huge heads and rounded backs rolling like the waves of the ocean and the ground shaking from the tramp of their feet. They stretched as far as the eye could see. Zeb was filled with amazement at the sight and wrote in his journal that he believed that there was sufficient big game in these parts to feed every Indian in the United States for a hundred years—if the animals were killed without waste.

Such a quantity of game excited his men, and some of them took to shooting buffalo just for the joy of it. Zebulon lectured them sternly about this.

"We hunt only for food," he said. "Never for pleasure. These beasts are not put here by Almighty God to be killed for sport."

Once, however, in need of meat, he and his men came upon a herd of buffalo and rode in among them with their muskets. A party of Pawnees spotted the herd at the same time and joined in the hunt. American soldiers and the wild redmen rode through the herd killing the buffalo they needed. Zebulon watched the Pawnees ride alongside the bulls and, using neither reins nor saddle, sink their arrows to the plume in the sides of the buffalo. He concluded that the bow and arrow was a better weapon for hunting buffalo than the service musket. Wounded by an arrow, the buffalo sank to the ground. Wounded by a bullet, the beast continued on and was often lost in the herd.

By mid-October they had reached the Arkansas River, and here the party was to split. Lieutenant Wilkinson was to go down the river, exploring it to its junction with the Mississippi. Zebulon was to go upstream, exploring to the source and then strike southward until he picked up the Red River, which he would descend to the Mississippi. He built two canoes for Lieutenant Wilkinson's party and on October twenty-eighth they parted. Wilkinson headed downstream taking with him four soldiers. Zebulon watched him until he had disappeared around a bend of the river, and then he himself headed due west, up the Arkansas River.

He now had with him, besides Dr. Robinson, fourteen men, among them Private Sparks. Pike was proud of all his men, but especially of John Sparks who was unfailingly self-reliant and willing. Among the soldiers Sparks was the best shot, and Zeb knew he would need his services in the weeks ahead.

Zebulon had thirty-five pounds of powder, forty pounds of lead and ten dozen cartridges. The lead would furnish about six hundred rounds when the cartridges were expended. For food the party would depend on what game it could kill, and so this small store of ammunition became of vital importance.

Winter was now approaching. For the past several days there had been lashing downpours of rain and violent thunderstorms. Now a cold wind boomed over the empty prairie, and on the day after the parting with Wilkinson two inches of snow fell. It was the first snow of the trip and did not lie long on the ground. Neither Zebulon nor anyone else in the party had any idea of the kind of weather to be met in midwinter in this territory. They reasoned that being so far south, approximately in the latitude of St. Louis, the winter would not be severe—certainly nowhere near as severe as that which they had endured in the headwaters of the Mississippi many hundreds of miles to the north.

Hence they were not equipped for a winter exploration. Their clothes were of cotton, and they carried a few blankets. That was the extent of their wardrobes. Watching the snow fall on that late October day, Zebulon wondered if this was merely a freak of the weather or if terrible days of below zero cold lay ahead. Whatever his conclusions, he kept them to himself.

The Arkansas River at the point where they started their exploration was too shallow for canoe travel so they went along the bank on their horses. The next day there was ice in the river, and the men were shivering in their cotton clothing when they awoke in the morning. A little farther upstream Pike came across the camp of the Spanish soldiers whose trail he had picked up among the Pawnees. He had heard of a route or trail from these parts leading to Santa Fe—the Santa Fe Trail—and they crossed it now. It was nothing more than a worn place over the surface of the prairie, and he would have liked to follow it, for knowledge of such a trail would be important in case of war with Spain—something that was never far from Zebulon's mind. But his instructions were to go up the Arkansas, and so he went on.

One day, standing on top of a rise to survey the country ahead through his telescope, he saw in the distance a huge herd of animals moving slowly northward.

"Horses," he shouted to Dr. Robinson. "Wild horses! Come on!" They jumped into their saddles and rode toward the herd. When they were about a quarter of a mile away, the herd discovered them.

Wheeling like a monstrous squadron of cavalry, the wild horses charged down upon them and then came to a stop only forty yards off. The thunder of their hooves made the whole prairie tremble. There were beautiful black and white stallions and grays among them.

Zebulon picked out a black stallion and tried to bring it down by "creasing." This meant putting a bullet across its neck just over the vertebra which would stun the animal without hurting it greatly. He missed, and immediately after he fired, the whole herd wheeled around and took off. But they did not go far.

The wild horses were puzzled and curious. Here were two horses, but on their backs were two men. Plainly they had never seen such a thing before. And so they wheeled about again and came back to eye Zebulon and the doctor. Neither Zebulon nor the doctor fired again, but just sat in their saddles, admiring the magnificence of the herd.

The next day, Zebulon decided to try and rope some of the mustangs, and made half a dozen lassos. He set out with a party of five and chased the mustangs for several miles, but captured none. They could get alongside them, but roping them was another matter, and the men returned to camp and laughed at their failure.

The rich earth of the prairies had now been replaced by a salty, sandy soil in which a thin spiky grass grew. Still game was plentiful. They came across herds of buffalos, deer, and elk, all on the move to winter pastures. Food was no problem. They dined on buffalo steaks every day, varying this diet with venison. But their horses did not fare so well. Grazing became more and more scarce, and two horses were finally so weak from hunger that they had to be turned loose.

Toward the middle of November they had left the area that was later to become the state of Kansas and were in what was to be Colorado. The prairies were behind and the ground was now broken and rocky.

On November fifteenth Pike was riding ahead of his party with Dr. Robinson when he saw off to his right what he took to be a small blue cloud. It was on the horizon and looked so strange that he reined in his horse and looked for a long time at it through his telescope.

"What is it?" asked Dr. Robinson.

"It looks like a blue cloud, even in the telescope," Zebulon replied. They rode on for a while, and then Zebulon suddenly realized what the "blue cloud" was.

It was a majestic mountain peak thrusting up against the sky like a tooth on the horizon. Below it he could now see small but distinct, a fringe of white. They were within sight of the Rocky Mountains, and the big peak he had seen was the one which was later to bear his name—Pike's Peak.

The men behind came up quickly and, topping the rise where Zebulon and Dr. Robinson had reined in their horses, sat gaping in silence for a moment at the grim sawtooth of mountains on the horizon with the forbidding blue peak rising above it.

Then with one accord they gave three cheers for the "Mexican Mountains" as they called them. They had come farther west than any other exploring party in this area. Lewis and Clark, traveling much farther north, had reached the Pacific. Zebulon Pike had pushed to the foot of the Rocky Mountains in the heart of Colorado.

But although Americans had not been this way before and the territory was for them unexplored, Zebulon and his party still came across the traces of the mysterious Spanish force that had penetrated deep into American territory.

One day, as they headed into the Rockies, they ran into a war party of Pawnees returning from an unsuccessful raid against the Comanches. There were sixty warriors in the party, and for a while it was touch and go whether the Pawnees would attack them.

A council was arranged, and Zeb distributed a few gifts from his stores. But the Pawnees demanded powder and bullets, and these Zebulon could not spare. He told them he could not give them ammunition. The Pawnees grew angry and threw away some of the gifts they had received. They started robbing the men, taking all the equipment they could lay their hands on.

Zebulon jumped on his horse and rode over to the chief. "If your men steal another single item from my soldiers," he said, "I will personally shoot the man who does it. You are their chief. Tell them so." The chieftain shouted the news to his warriors, and the Indians slunk off. But they managed to take with them an ax and a sword and several pieces of baggage, and Zebulon had too few men to go after them and punish them.

On the next day Zebulon decided that he must try to climb the blue mountain peak which now loomed much larger. He decided not to take his whole party but to build a stockade where his men would be safe from further attacks by the Pawnees.

When the stockade was built, he struck up one fork of the Arkansas to the north which seemed to rise in the blue mountain peak that so fascinated him. This fork was actually Fountain Creek. Zebulon thought that when he got to the top of the huge mountain, he would be able to see the whole course of the river.

He built the stockade on the bank of the river. The landward side was protected by breastworks five feet high. The stockade was the first American structure erected in Colorado, and over it the American flag was raised for the first time in this territory. The site was the present city of Pueblo.

The stockade was soon finished and on the same day Zebulon set out with Dr. Robinson and two soldiers to ascend the river to the north and then climb the big peak. Another mountain lay between them and the peak, but in the clear air it seemed that they would certainly be at the foot of this mountain by evening. By nightfall they had not yet reached it and had to camp in the open.

The next day the party set out again. But again the clear air, making distant objects seem very near, deceived Zebulon. By evening he had gone twenty-two miles and had only reached the base of the first mountain. Nonetheless, he was sure that on the following day he would be able to climb it and the blue peak also, make his observations, and descend again by nightfall.

Accordingly, on the following morning they left the blankets in the camp and set out, carrying no baggage.

They climbed all day and found the going far rougher than they had anticipated. In places they had to scale perpendicular rocks, climbing on each other's shoulders, the last man being hauled up by those who had reached the top. They fell constantly on the loose stones. The day was clear, but below them the world was blotted out by a snowstorm. That night they slept without blankets in a cave on the side of the mountain.

The next morning Pike was up early. From the mouth of the cave he could see below him an ocean of cloud, "wave piled on wave and foaming," and above a perfect blue sky. But it had snowed during the night, and the snow now lay thick on the mountainside.

Pike, clad only in cotton shirt and pants, struggled up to the summit of the mountain, and standing there, up to his waist in snow, found that the big peak he sought was still sixteen miles away and as high up again as he had climbed already. Its sides glittered with snow and ice. It would take two, perhaps three days of plowing through the snow, with the temperature below zero, to reach the summit.

Wearily he turned and looked at Dr. Robinson, who shook his head. They couldn't make it. The huge mountain was beyond their reach. He had first seen it as a blue cloud a hundred and fifty miles away. It had lured him this far, and now he could not reach it. He gave the peak one last, hungry look and then turned without a word and led the way back.

Pike's Peak would never be climbed by Zebulon Montgomery Pike from whom it took its name.

CHAPTER ELEVEN

Trapped in the Rockies

CHAPTER ELEVEN

ZEBULON PIKE and his men were now in mountainous country down whose gorges and valleys there flowed a labyrinth of rivers. This area was unknown territory, and even the task of tracing the Arkansas to its source became next to impossible. So many tributaries flowed into the Arkansas that Pike could not decide which was the real river and which the stream flowing into it.

He was actually in the front range of the Rockies at the Continental Divide. In these mountains rose many rivers and their tributaries that flowed into the Mississippi and others that flowed into the Gulf of California. Among them were the South Platte River, with four major tributaries, the North Platte, the Little Snake, the White, and the Colorado.

Many times Zebulon split his party, sending one group up one river while he went up another. The cold was intense and game was scarce. The horses were starving and could carry no load. At one camp in this desolate region flocks of hungry birds swooped down, so ravenous that they pecked at the sores and galls on the horses' backs. They even settled on the shoulders and arms of the men and snatched food from their hands.

The terrible winter of the Rockies had now begun in earnest. It snowed constantly. The wind howled around the empty mountain peaks, booming and screaming through the gorges. The men's moccasins had worn out and they had to make others of buffalo hides. They cut up their blankets to make clothing and then had to lie without covering on the ground, shivering in sub-zero weather at night, trying to get some sleep. Many times they had to ford rivers in which the water did not freeze because it moved through the gorges so quickly.

But as soon as they crossed these cold rivers, the men's clothing froze stiff in the howling wind. It was not long before almost all the men in the party had frozen toes or feet. Still they hobbled about—up one river, across a mountain to find another river, down this one, back again, trying to get a picture of the area and the waters that flowed through it.

After several weeks of exploring in the Rockies, Pike believed that he had found the headwaters of the Arkansas —one of the purposes of his journey. His object now was to find the Red River and descend it to the Mississippi.

He believed that the Red River had its source some where in the area he was exploring because the plains Indians he met had referred many times to a river called the Colorado. "Colorado" is Spanish for "red color." Plainly, he reasoned, this Colorado was the Red River he was seeking.

But the truth was that the Colorado was a different

river altogether and emptied, not into the Mississippi, but into the Gulf of Mexico, and the Red River rose many miles to the south and east.

The story of the Colorado (Red) River which he had heard from the Indians, kept Pike long in the Rockies. He knew that the river he was looking for must flow in a southeasterly direction. Finally he came across a river that flowed in the right direction and believed that he had at last reached the Red River. Down this he would descend to the Mississippi.

On Christmas eve in 1806 his party had been without food for two days, but they now found and shot eight buffalo—an enormously welcome Christmas present. The men cut up the hides to make moccasins, but the untanned skin was next to useless for this purpose. However, they had food, and they ate a huge meal of roasted buffalo meat. Then they lay shivering in the snow, one side of them burning from the fire, the other freezing.

Christmas Day was spent trying to dry some of the buffalo meat over the fire. Meat was now all they had to eat. The supplies of beans and flour were long exhausted. They had not even any salt, and the lack of this weakened them. The horses were so weak that they could scarcely stand. They fell repeatedly, cutting their legs. To ease their work, Zeb built a sledge, but the ground was so rough that the sledge was soon broken.

Hobbling on frozen feet, the men carried most of the load of buffalo meat, powder, and shot. Zeb saw to it that, even though he was the smallest man in the party, his pack was as big as the rest.

He decided that he had gained a good picture of the maze of rivers rising in the Rockies and that the salvation of his party now lay in getting out of the terrible trap of the mountains and into the prairies. He believed that he

had found the Red River at last, and so he announced
that fact to his men.

"We are on our way home," he told them. Despite
their frozen feet, hands, and faces, they managed to grin
at one another.

But the going became increasingly hard. It was as if
the mountains were determined to hold them prisoner.

The river flowed through a great gorge, whose sides
were so steep that the men had constantly to cross from
one bank to the other to find a wide enough place on which
to travel.

In swift-flowing areas, where the water was moving too
fast to freeze, this meant floundering across the river with
the water up to their waists and sometimes up to their
shoulders. They dragged the starving horses with them,
even though they were themselves loaded down with packs
weighing seventy pounds on their backs. Their frozen
feet were almost a blessing, for they could not feel the
rocks of the river bed nor the cold bite of the water.
Where the river widened and the water was frozen, horses
and men fell constantly on the ice. The horses were hor-
ribly bruised and cut, and after each fall they could
scarcely get on their feet again. When a horse could not
rise, the men hauled it on its side across the ice.

The going was painfully slow. On December twenty-
ninth they made five miles; December thirtieth, eight
miles; December thirty-first, four miles.

On New Year's Day, 1807, when the party was nearing
the end of its strength and was still locked in the mountains, Zebulon decided to climb a nearby peak to survey
the land ahead. He toiled up in a blizzard, but when he
got to the top, the weather moderated, and in the moon-
light he could see the prairies ahead. A few miles more
and they would be out of the mountains.

He hurried back to the camp and woke the men. "The prairie is only a few miles away," he said. "Two days travel at the most, and we will be out of the mountains."

The men cheered this news, and even before it was daylight, they started out on what was now almost a flight for life. In their weakened condition, however, they could go only slowly. The river still flowed through the wild gorge with rocks on either side and rapids in the center. There was a margin of ice on the shore of the river, and Zebulon put eight of his men to building sledges that could be hauled along this. He himself decided to quit the river with the miserable horses and go over the mountains downstream.

He argued that the horses would at least be able to get a footing on the rocks of the mountain, instead of falling constantly on the ice. But the horses were weaker than Zeb had estimated. One fell over a precipice and bruised itself so badly that it had to be shot to end its suffering. Two others fell also and were in such pain that they could go no farther. Zebulon decided that though they might recover, it would be sheer cruelty to bring them farther. There was a little grazing in the area provided by the branches of firs and spruce. He set the horses loose and left them, giving them a chance to work out their own salvation.

Meanwhile the men had built the sledges and started down the river, pulling them along the ice at the banks. But they met several precipices and with picks and shovels had to build ramps of earth, rocks, snow, and ice to get the sledges down these.

In the life and death struggle to get out of the mountains, Zeb now had to divide his party. He sent Dr. Robinson and one soldier ahead to hunt for game. Nobody had had anything to eat for twenty-four hours. Eight soldiers in parties of two, struggled along with four sledges. Another party of three men was put in charge of the remaining horses with instructions to get them unloaded downriver out of the mountains. Meanwhile, Zebulon, who was the best shot, also went off in search of game.

For five miles Zeb went downriver through the immense gorge. By nightfall he came to a place where the walls of the gorge were perpendicular and the river plunged over a fall. The doctor, he knew, was ahead of him, and so also was one of the parties of soldiers with a sledge. He wondered how they had got past this part and looked around for the road they had taken.

As he looked about him, he saw one of the soldiers who was in charge of a sledge, climbing one of the perpendicular sides of the gorge. Zeb called to him. The soldier and his buddy joined Zeb and said they had had nothing to eat for two days. That night they proposed to boil a deerskin to make some kind of broth for their supper.

Zebulon found a ravine up the side of the gorge. The bottom of the ravine was filled with ice. Zebulon and the two soldiers clawed their way up with the stores from the sledge.

At the top Zebulon left the men and went to search for game. He shot a deer, but to his surprise he only wounded it, and the animal got away in the dark. Zebulon came back to camp. There he found that the soldiers had left the deerskin they were going to boil for supper down by the river. But they were all too exhausted to go after it; so they contented themselves with handfuls of snow for dinner and spent the night huddled over a fire.

The next day Zeb was out early after game. It was his birthday and he was now twenty-eight years of age. He hoped he was going to be lucky and for a while it seemed that he would be. He came upon deer after deer, but though he took careful aim and managed to control his shivering, he only succeeded in wounding the animals, and they all got away.

What was the matter? He had brought down rocketing pheasants with this same gun, and now he could not kill a deer with it.

He looked the gun over carefully and discovered the trouble. The barrel was slightly bent due to the rough treatment it had received in the struggle to get out of the mountains. He returned to camp and picked up a double-barreled gun, assuring the men that after the first kill he would return immediately with food for them.

He climbed to the top of a mountain in his search for game and then made a disastrous discovery. He could see the river ahead and the prairies, but several features of the landscape appeared familiar.

He was not on the Red River after all! He was on the Arkansas, the same river on which he had traveled upstream. In the maze of rivers in the mountains he had completely lost his way and, having made a circle, had come back to the Arkansas River. It was a bitter blow, but at least he now knew the true course of the Arkansas into the Rockies, and he had discovered also the source of the Platte River.

But where the Red River rose was still a mystery. Wearily Zebulon went down the mountain toward the river and at the foot found the three men he had sent ahead with the horses. They had some good news for him, for they had killed a buffalo and some deer.

Zebulon sent them back to the soldiers, who were waiting for him. Then he collected the straggling elements of his party together again. Dr. Robinson, he found, had been ill for two days—holed up in the mountains and unable to hunt. He had been poisoned by some berries he had eaten. The other men came in by ones and twos and by January ninth the party was reunited. Several deer and buffalo were shot, and they were no longer faced with starvation. But Zebulon faced the harsh fact that he had so far failed in one major aim of his expedition—finding the source of the Red River and traveling down it to the Mississippi.

What should he do? The winter was at its height; a winter far more severe than he had reckoned on enduring. The men's clothes were worn to shreds. There was not a pair of boots in the whole company. The horses were exhausted and useless as pack animals. While his men feasted on buffalo meat around the fire, Zebulon went off by himself and thought the matter out.

The conclusion he came to was the only one acceptable to a soldier. He must leave the Arkansas River and strike south into the mountains to find the Red River. That was what he had been ordered to do. Therefore that was what he must do. But he would not take the horses with him. Instead he decided to build a small fort on the site of what is now Canyon City, Colorado, and leave two men there with the horses. He would send for them when he had found the Red River. He would leave them powder and shot and what stores he could spare and with the rest of the men go on in search of the Red River.

Once his mind was made up, the fort was soon built. Baroney, the interpreter, and Private Patrick Smith were left there with the horses. The rest struck south into the unexplored mountains, each man, including Zebulon, carrying a seventy-pound pack on his back.

Again they ran into bad luck. They came across several small herds of buffalo, wintering in the mountain but the buffalo were distant and the men's muskets were of such small caliber that they could not kill any of them. Several times they wounded animals, but they always got away.

The supply of meat they had brought with them was soon exhausted. When they had been two days without food, though there was plenty of game around, Zebulon and Dr. Robinson, the two best shots in the party, went out to hunt, determined that they would not return until they had made a kill. They left the rest of the men in a camp. Nine of them had frozen feet and could scarcely hobble around.

On January 19, 1807, Zebulon and Dr. Robinson had been four days without food and had spent two nights sleeping in the open without blankets to cover them. They were so weak they could hardly walk and were overcome with frequent attacks of nausea. Yet Zebulon was determined not to return to his men empty-handed.

"I'd rather die out here in the snow alone," he told Dr. Robinson, "than face my men and tell them I haven't been able to get any food for them."

Suddenly, against the shimmering white snow, they saw a dark patch moving toward them. Buffalo! But they were out of range. His head swimming with weakness, Zebulon forced himself to run half a mile toward the herd. When he reached a clump of cedar, he steadied his rifle against the trunk of a tree, sighted on a bull and fired. The animal went down, but was on its feet again in a second. Dr. Robinson fired, and the buffalo staggered, but still went on. Zebulon had a double-barreled gun with him and fired another round. The bull went down on its knees and rolled over on its side—dead. At last—after four days of fasting—the men would have food.

The two quickly cut off as much of the flesh as they could carry and, without pausing to eat, stumbled back to the camp. They had twelve miles to go. And fell many times under their loads. But at last they reached the little fort, arriving at midnight.

Zebulon staggered into the firelight around which his

men were crouched and dropped his load of buffalo meat. He immediately fell on top of it, fainting from weakness.

When he had recovered and all the men had eaten, he asked the sergeant who had been left in charge what his thoughts had been, left alone four days without food, with his commanding officer gone.

"Well, sir," said the sergeant, "I knew if there was game to be had, you'd get it and bring it in. But I decided that if you hadn't returned by tomorrow, I'd take some of the men whose feet are not too badly frozen and go looking for you in case you were hurt out there."

"Were you beginning to give up hope?" asked Zeb.

The sergeant looked around at the men. Their feet were wrapped in frozen tatters of buffalo hide, and their fingers were swollen like sausages and split down the backs from frostbite. "We decided, given our choice," he said, "that we'd sooner fight the whole Pawnee nation than go through this again. Of course," he added, "what's got to be endured has got to be endured. But given a choice of a way to die, cold and starvation aren't what I'd choose."

The next day Zebulon sent the doctor and two of the men whose feet were not too badly frozen after the remains of the buffalo. Then he took the bandages of buffalo hides and rags off the feet of the other men and examined them. John Sparks, the cheerful soldier who had gone with Zeb up to the headwaters of the Mississippi, was in the worst condition. His feet were white as marble and swollen so badly that his ankles were as big as his calves, and his toes were little balls of white on the ends of his foot. One other man, Thomas Dougherty, was in a similar condition. Both were in danger of having to have their feet amputated. Zebulon shook his head. These men could go no farther. They would have to be left behind.

Zebulon explained the situation to Sparks. "We have to

go on, John. And we have to leave you and Dougherty here. I'll send back for you as soon as I have found a trail to the Red River. I'll leave you all the stores and plenty of ammunition. But you can't come with us."

"I think I could go a mile or two more," said Sparks. "I can still walk and it doesn't hurt. I can't feel anything in my feet. It's just like they weren't there."

Zebulon shook his head. "You'll have to stay," he said.

For the first time Sparks broke down. "Please let us come, sir," he said. "Even if it kills us, we don't want to stay here alone in the wilderness." There were tears in his eyes and tears on Zeb's face too. He had come to love this soldier who had borne every hardship without a word of complaint. And now he had to leave him.

"I can't take you, John," Zeb said. "I have to think of the other men. They all have frozen feet but not as bad as yours. You have to think of your comrades, and give them a chance of getting to safety. We couldn't make a mile a day taking you and Dougherty with us. That could mean death for everyone. I have to get them to safety. That is the way it is for a soldier. I give you my word I'll get you back."

"All right, sir," said Sparks and lowered his head to hide his tears, for he was ashamed of them.

A stockade was built for Sparks and Dougherty, and they were left with stores, ammunition, and all that was left of the buffalo meat.

Zebulon set off south with the remainder of the party. He turned once to look back. Dougherty and Sparks, supporting themselves on sticks, were standing outside the stockade, tiny figures in the distance.

Zeb waved, and across the silent, empty snowfields, the sound of a faint cheer reached him from the two soldiers.

CHAPTER TWELVE

Strange Horsemen

CHAPTER TWELVE

Striking southward, hunting for the elusive Red River, Zebulon Pike soon came face to face with the Sangre de Cristo (Blood of Christ) Mountains.

He called them the White Mountains and was appalled by their height and their grim, menacing, ice-covered precipices. Food was again the great problem—the problem that had to be immediately solved, for they carried only enough meat for one meal, having left the rest with Sparks and Dougherty. Zeb told the men to head for a clump of pines he could see at the foot of the Sangre de Cristo Mountains while he and Dr. Robinson went out to hunt.

Ammunition was now very low. If it ran out, all of them would starve, and so every round had to be made to count. The two had hardly left the men before a blizzard sprang up. They could see only a few feet ahead of them. Hunting was impossible. They rejoined the men, stumbling forward through three feet of snow and finding their way by compass.

The party was now on the high prairies, at the foot of the Sangre de Cristo Mountains, and it was plain that all the game had left the flatlands and gone into the mountains to shelter in the valleys during the winter.

Zebulon decided to strike into the mountains, both to hunt for game and to see if he could find a pass through the mountains, for he believed that the Red River must lie somewhere on the other side of them. He set out alone and floundered on in his worn clothes and tatters of moccasins until the snow became so deep that he could go no farther. For the first time now he became discouraged. The lives of all the men lay in his hands. He had no food for them. Game was scarce. He had only a few rounds of ammunition left. And he was caught in the terrible trap of the winter. When he got back to camp to report that the mountains were impassable at this point, even Dr. Robinson hadn't a cheery word. The men said nothing, but went to bed in the snow without food. They were two days on their way and had had but one meal.

The next day the men started grumbling. They had been through hardships almost impossible to bear and they had borne them. Now they cracked. One of them complained aloud that they had had nothing to eat for three days, were made to march through snow up to their waists, and had to carry packs under which a horse would stumble.

Zeb heard the remark, for it was intentionally made loud enough for him to hear. But he decided to say nothing for the present. They went on in silence, struggling, floundering, slipping, and shivering. Zebulon went ahead to break the trail. He carried as big a pack as any of the men, and, breaking the trail, pushing into the

deep snow, he had the hardest work. But he felt that this
was the least he could do to hearten his men.

Then he heard Dr. Robinson shout, "Look! Look
there!" He pointed over to the west. A line of black dots
against the snow revealed a small herd of buffalo. The
two dropped their heavy packs immediately and unslung
their rifles. Dr. Robinson was in better physical condition
than Zeb and ran ahead until he got behind a small hill.
From this spot he sighted on a bull and fired. The bull
crumpled to the ground—dead.

The two ran to the fallen buffalo and resting their rifles
on its back, shot three more. All was done in a matter of
minutes and then the herd scattered. Zeb and Robinson
cut chunks of the steaming meat from one of the Buffalo
and brought it back to the men, who had camped by a little
belt of trees. The men had a fire going, but they were so
ravenous that they cut lumps of the raw meat and ate them
without cooking.

When they had eaten their fill, Zebulon called the
soldier who had grumbled about the hardships of the
march. The others looked anxiously at Zebulon, remembering how harsh a disciplinarian he was. What the soldier had said, though pardonable in the circumstances,
could be taken as sedition—as an attempt to incite the men
to mutiny. And in those days, many men had been shot
for saying less.

"Brown," said Zebulon, "I heard you grumbling on the
trail yesterday. I want to ask you some questions. Who
is the smallest man in this party, Brown, in size?"

"You, sir, I reckon," said Brown.

"That is right," said Zeb. "And I am your officer. Now,
have you seen me keep aside food for myself when you and
the others had nothing to eat?"

"No, sir."

"Have you seen me taking my ease around the fire while you and the others were struggling in the snow, hunting?"

"No, sir."

"Have you seen me carrying a lighter pack than any of the men in the party?"

"No, sir. Your pack weighs as much as anybody's."

"Good," said Zeb. "Yet, it is you who were grumbling and not me. I, as your officer, have to do more than you. I am the smallest man in the party, but I break trail for you and hunt for you and carry a seventy-pound pack on my back as well. You have to walk only the day's march, but I have to do the day's march plus eight or ten miles more hunting. You should be ashamed of yourself for grumbling—ashamed of yourself as a man and ashamed of yourself as a soldier. You have had less to do than your own officer."

"I'm sorry, sir," said Brown. "I was cold and hungry and didn't think I could go on any more. . . ."

"And so were we all," said Zebulon. "But instead of helping your comrades by being cheerful, you spread your own discouragement to them and added to their load. You've been a good soldier, Brown, and I am going to overlook the fault this time. But remember that a soldier isn't just himself. He is all the other men who are with him as well. His responsibility is not just to himself. It is to them first and to himself last. Remember that, and don't let me hear another word of complaint out of you."

"No, sir," said Brown. "I'm sorry, and it won't happen again."

After this interview, Dr. Robinson took Zebulon aside and asked him whether he had not been too hard on the man in taking note of his fault.

"No," said Zeb. "If you once let a soldier pity himself,

he isn't a soldier anymore. And that goes from the general to the drummer boy."

Before turning in that night Zebulon, with Dr. Robinson, again examined his men's feet. He found one of the men—Private Menaugh—could not possibly go on. His legs were frozen almost to the knees.

"Have you been treating your feet?" asked Dr. Robinson.

"Don't do no good, sir," said Menaugh. "I've been rubbing them with snow, but I can't feel nothing in them. And my hands get so cold, I can't rub my feet for long."

"You'll have to stay here," said Zeb gently. "We'll build a shelter for you and leave you some stores and come back and get you. If you try to go on any farther, you'll lose your legs."

"Yes, sir," said Menaugh. "I was expecting that. Do you reckon I'll be alone here a long time, sir?"

"Not one minute longer than I can help," said Zeb. "That's a promise."

They spent the next two days drying the buffalo meat because with ammunition so low and game getting scarcer, Zebulon was determined to carry as much meat as he could. There was plenty, so they left a large supply for Menaugh, together with a musket and ammunition, and then set off again.

Now their luck changed. The blizzards of the last three days ceased and though the snow was still three feet deep, they made fourteen miles. They came to a small creek flowing east which Zebulon believed might be the headwaters of the Red River. He followed it for some distance through a ravine and saw, ahead and to the west, another range of mountains. He had no idea what mountains these were, but continued on toward them.

Then he came upon a belt of trees with strange marks painted on them. He was, then, in country previously explored, but not by Americans. Could the marks, he wondered, have been made by that mysterious party of six hundred Spaniards whose trail he had lost in the Rockies to the north? Following the ravine through which the creek flowed, Zebulon was actually cutting westward across the Sangre de Cristo Range. Soon the party was no longer climbing, but going down hill. On the right was a huge area covered entirely by enormous sand dunes. Whipped by winds for thousands of years, the dunes resembled an ocean in a storm. While the men made camp, Zeb climbed to the top of one of the dunes and examined the country ahead through his telescope. He came running back to the camp, highly excited.

"There's a big river over there!" he shouted. "And it flows in the right direction—to the south and east!"

"The Red River!" the men shouted and started cheering. They were saved at last. They had got out of the mountains and were close to the banks of the river that would carry them back to the Mississippi and their homes. Two days later they had reached the banks of the river, but not before they had made a strange discovery. Going ahead of his men as usual with Dr. Robinson, Zebulon stopped suddenly and pointed to some barely visible marks in the sand.

"Horses," he said and the two exchanged glances.

Horses in this wilderness? Whose horses? Indians'? Or those of the Spanish cavalry that had penetrated so deeply into American territory?

Zebulon had no answer, but again he wondered whether war had broken out between the United States and Spain in the months since he had left St. Louis. The situation had been extremely touchy when he left, and his orders had said that he was to avoid contact or hostilities with the Spanish should he meet them. The tracks of the horses in the sands of what was later to become the Great Sand Dunes National Monument in Colorado gave him a lot to think about. But he could make neither head nor tail of the puzzle.

The place where they struck the river, after crossing the sand dunes, was barren of trees, and on the following day they went downstream about eighteen miles, searching for timber. Here they found a tributary flowing into the river from the west bank. They crossed over and, after going up the tributary for a few miles, found an excellent grove of trees. Here then would be timber with which to build a fort and also boats to go downstream to the Mississippi.

Zebulon decided a fort would be necessary. He had good reason. His party was now very small, reduced to eleven men, including himself and Dr. Robinson, for five had been left on the back trail. The men were weak and would need a chance to recuperate before going downstream. And he had still to send back for the men he had left behind. He was short of ammunition. He would have to lay in a store of food before going down the river. These and many other considerations demanded that he build a fort in case of attack by Indians or by the mysterious horsemen, possibly Spanish, whose trail he had come across in the sand dunes.

Zebulon personally laid out the plans for the fort the day after their arrival on the river. While the men worked at felling logs and building the stockade, he and Dr. Robinson explored the surrounding country. They found themselves in a paradise—an immense, well-watered prairie perhaps sixty miles in length—that lay between two great mountain ranges. There was an abundance of deer. Herds could be seen grazing all over the prairie, and in places the river was dotted with islands. One of these Zeb reckoned contained a hundred thousand acres of meadowland.

But the river was frozen and could not be descended for some weeks, even if boats were available. The men were almost all crippled from exposure, and the five left on the back trail must be rescued. The task of hunting deer and bringing the carcasses back four and five miles, and even farther, as the herds moved away from the hunters, would prove more and more formidable.

Somewhere to the south and west, Zebulon suspected, was the Spanish city of Santa Fe. Help could be had there, but he, as a soldier, could not cross into Spanish territory. The unwritten laws of nations demanded that any exploring party in distress be given supplies, irrespective of nationality. But suppose that the United States was at war with Spain? If he himself went to Santa Fe for more powder and bullets and clothing, he would be taken prisoner.

He decided, therefore, that since Dr. Robinson was a civilian, he should be the one to go to the Spanish city to get relief for Zebulon's party. On the following day the doctor set out. Meanwhile, Zebulon sent a corporal and four men back along the trail to contact Menaugh, Dougherty, and Sparks and bring them in if they were able to make the journey.

With Dr. Robinson gone and the corporal and four men headed back to the rescue of those who had been left behind, Zebulon had only four men with him. Of these, two were suffering from frozen feet. These men worked on the fort while Zeb went out hunting, for on his skill alone depended their food supply.

One day in the middle of February, a week after the doctor had left, Zebulon was out hunting with one of the men when he saw two horsemen riding over the summit of a hill half a mile away. Uncertain who they might be, he tried to escape from them. But they immediately charged at him with lances raised. When he and the soldier with him turned to face them, the horsemen wheeled around and made off. Then they turned again.

Finally, Zebulon ducked into a ravine and told the soldier to stand ready to fire. The horsemen were obviously hunting them. He hoped that he could lure them near enough to talk to them, and in the ravine he and the soldier would be safe from being run down and skewered on the lances. The two mysterious horsemen, hunting cautiously around the rocks, finally got to the mouth of the ravine, and Zebulon called out to them. They immediately whirled around.

"Put down your musket and go out to them," Zebulon told the soldier. "I'll cover you from behind."

Zebulon then shouted that he was an American and a friend. The horsemen approached cautiously. One was a Spanish cavalryman and the other an Indian in the service of the Spanish.

"Where are you from?" Zebulon asked.

"Santa Fe," was the reply. "Your friend, Dr. Robinson, has arrived there and been well received. What are your plans?"

Zebulon suspected, however, from the way the two horsemen had charged him and the soldier that they were spies, come to estimate the strength of his force. In the back of his mind was always the uneasy possibility that the United States and Spain were at war. Therefore, when he was asked what his plans were, he replied merely that when the river thawed and he had built some boats, he was going down it to its junction with the Mississippi at Natchitoches. He said the two could accompany him to his fort. There they were surprised to find so few men and could not believe that Zebulon and his party had come through the mountains without horses.

The next day the two horsemen left, saying that they would report to the Spanish governor, whose name was Allencaster, in Santa Fe. Zebulon redoubled work on the fort, suspecting that the Spanish might decide to raid it to prevent him from descending the river. That evening the corporal he had sent to the relief of the men on the back trail returned. He brought Private Hugh Menaugh with him.

"What about Sparks and Dougherty?" Zebulon asked. "Are they able to travel?"

For an answer the corporal gave a little piece of buffalo hide to Zebulon. Zeb opened it and found inside some small bones. They were the toes of the two men, Dougherty and Sparks, whose feet were now reduced to stumps from frostbite.

"They begged that you not leave them to perish in the mountains," the corporal reported. "They cannot walk, and they were in despair when I left them to report back to you."

"They will not be left," said Zebulon. "I will get them back to their homes, if it is my last act on earth."

Accused of Spying

CHAPTER THIRTEEN

T HE NEXT DAY Zebulon sent Sergeant William Meek and Private Theodore Miller back to get the men with the frostbitten feet. Their instructions were to cross the mountains to the Arkansas River and find Baroney, the interpreter, and the soldier who had been left with him in charge of the horses. They were to bring them, with such horses as were in good shape, back through the mountains, picking up Sparks and Dougherty, who would be able to make the journey on horseback.

Meek and Miller carried ten pounds of venison in their packs and a few cartridges. They had volunteered for the work. They would have to trek two hundred miles across two great mountain ranges in midwinter, through unexplored territory with only a compass to guide them. But their spirit was such that they thought themselves honored to be chosen for the rescue expedition. Zebulon went several miles with them to set them on their way and then turned back. The two men were soon out of sight.

He was worried now about the Spaniards. The cavalryman and the Indian had left to report to the Spanish governor in Santa Fe. He could then expect another visit from a larger party of Spaniards. He hoped they would come with supplies, but he could not be sure of this so he posted a lookout on top of a hill all day. At night he manned the bastion of the little fort he had constructed and over which the Stars and Stripes now flew. The next several days were spent in watching and hunting. Zebulon many times came across the hoof prints of horses. There had been large parties of horsemen in this country recently.

On February 26, 1807, the sentinel on the hill fired a warning gun, and soon two Frenchmen appeared at the fort.

"We have been sent by Governor Allencaster," they said. "He has news that the Ute Indians are planning to attack you, and he is sending a party of fifty Spanish dragoons to you to prevent the Indian attack. They will be here soon."

Fifty Spanish dragoons! That was an enormous force—far more than was needed to ward off an Indian attack in this open country, with a good fort to fight from. Zebulon was suspicious, but said nothing. A little while later a huge body of horsemen appeared. There were not only fifty dragoons but also fifty mounted militiamen, armed with lances, sabers, and pistols. A body of one hundred horsemen! As soon as they were in sight, Zebulon ordered his men to man the ramparts of his little fort. There was only a handful of men, and most of them were crippled by frostbite. But they were hardened soldiers and ready to sell their lives dearly.

Zebulon turned to one of the Frenchmen. "Go out and tell the commander of that Spanish troop to leave his men in the woods over there," he said. "I will meet him midway between our two forces. If he brings his men on, we'll fire."

The Frenchman agreed, and Zeb, armed only with his sword, went out to meet the leaders of the troop. There were two—Don Ignacio Saltelo and Don Bartholomew Fernandez, both having the rank of lieutenant.

"Do you come in peace or war?" asked Zebulon.

"In peace," replied Don Ignacio.

"Our countries are not at war?"

"No."

Much relieved, Zebulon invited the two officers into the fort for breakfast. They breakfasted on deer meat and exchanged only small talk during the meal, for Spanish courtesy demanded that no business be discussed at the table. When breakfast was over, Don Ignacio got down to brass tacks.

"The Governor of New Mexico," he said, "has learned that you have missed your way in the mountains and has ordered me to offer you, in his name, mules, horses, money, or whatever you need to get to the head of the Red River."

"The Red River?" cried Zebulon. "But isn't this the Red River?"

The Spaniard smiled. "No, señor," he replied, "this is not the Red River. That is far to the east and south of here. You are on the Rio del Norte (the Rio Grande)."

"The Rio del Norte!" cried Zebulon. If this was true he was deep in Spanish territory and had erected a fort and raised the American flag on Spanish land. He immediately ordered the Stars and Stripes flying over the top of his little fort to be lowered.

"Governor Allencaster in Santa Fe, as I have said," con-

tinued Don Ignacio, "is willing to supply you with whatever you need to get to the Red River. However, he wants
you first to come to Sante Fe. You will understand that he
would like to have an explanation of what you are doing
with an armed force on the Spanish frontier."

What was this? A trap to get him to Santa Fe, where
he would be taken prisoner?

"My orders will not permit me to go deeper into Spanish territory," replied Zebulon. "Furthermore, I have
some men who are frostbitten on the back trail, and I have
sent a sergeant and a man to get them in. I will not leave
until they return."

"I have no orders to force you to come to Santa Fe," replied Don Ignacio gently. "We are not enemies. But I
think you will agree that the govenor is entitled to an
explanation of your presence on Spanish territory. You
can wait if you wish until your men are brought in. If,
however, you will come to Santa Fe with me now, I will
send an escort of my cavalrymen into the mountains to
rescue the other members of your party, and they will rejoin you in Santa Fe."

The offer seemed genuine. Zebulon was anxious about
the fate of Dougherty and Sparks. Not only were they his
soldiers, but he was particularly fond of Sparks and had
pledged his word that he would not leave him to perish
in the wilderness. Added to this, he had explicit orders not
to antagonize any Spanish force he might meet on his
journeys. If he refused to go, it would mean bloodshed—
an engagement between American and Spanish soldiers,
deep in Spanish territory. This would be very embarrassing to the government in Washington.

"All right," he said. "I will go with you to Santa Fe.
And you will have your dragoons wait here for my sergeant
and help him bring in the rest of the men if need be. Then

you will bring them all on to Santa Fe. But I will have
to give my sergeant written orders to come to the city and
leave a couple of my men here to meet him, otherwise he
will not believe your men and will think I have been taken
prisoner or killed."

He wrote the orders for Sergeant Meek and then told
his men that the Spaniards were friends and they were
to go to Santa Fe with them. The men did not like the
idea. They distrusted the Spanish and suspected treachery.
However, they went out of the fort and the Spanish cavalry,
seeing their miserable clothing and ragged shoes, presented them with blankets and moccasins.

A week later Zebulon was in Santa Fe, interviewing
Governor Allencaster. Meanwhile he had solved the mystery of the huge party of Spanish horses that had penetrated deep into American territory to the Arkansas River.
They had been sent under a Lieutenant Malgares especially to keep an eye on Pike and his men. Spain was fearful that Pike's expedition was in reality a hostile move
against Spanish territory and not merely an attempt to
explore the Louisiana Purchase frontiers.

Governor Allencaster was cold and hostile during his
first interview with Zebulon. "You came to spy in our
country, did you not?" he demanded almost as soon as
they met.

"No," said Zebulon. "I came to find the extent of
my own country."

"What is your official position?" demanded the governor.

"I am an officer of the United States Army," replied
Zebulon.

"What about this Dr. Robinson? Is he a member of
your party?"

The question was embarrassing for Zebulon. Robinson

was a civilian. He could be shot as a spy if Zebulon said he was working for the United States Army. The doctor was not actually, officially a member of the party, having joined it at St. Louis as a volunteer.

"No," Zebulon replied. "Dr. Robinson is not a member of my party."

"Do you know him?"

"Yes. He is from St. Louis."

"How many men have you?" asked the governor.

"Fifteen," replied Zebulon.

"And Dr. Robinson makes sixteen," said the governor.

"I have told you that Dr. Robinson is not a member of my party," replied Zebulon. He was trying to cover up for the doctor by disassociating him from the party, lest he be treated as a civilian spy. "I will not answer any more questions about Dr. Robinson."

That concluded the first interview. Zebulon was told to return that evening to the governor, bringing his papers with him. His reception had not been friendly, as he had been promised. It had been distinctly hostile, and all the promises of help he had received from the two Spanish lieutenants at his fort were plainly false. But now it was too late to alter the situation. He was in the hands of the Spaniards, and only a bold front would save him.

When he returned to see the governor again that night, His Excellency was still cold toward him. The governor started his questions again. "Where were you born?" he demanded.

Zebulon lost his temper. "I have told you that I am an officer of the United States Army," he said. "You will find all the details concerning me on my commission. Here it is."

The Governor could not speak English so Zebulon translated the commission into French, which was the only language they had in common. The governor's attitude immediately changed. He rose and extended his hand and said that he was glad to make the acquaintance of a gentleman. But Zebulon was not deceived. The next day, far from being released, the governor told Zebulon that he must go to Chihuahua to be questioned by the commandant general there.

Zebulon decided there and then to put an end to the fencing. "Am I and my men being taken to Chihuahua as prisoners of war?" he demanded.

"Not at all," said the governor.

"You have disarmed my men without my knowledge or my consent," continued Zebulon. "Are their arms to be returned to them or not?"

"They can have them back at any time," said the governor, flustered by the boldness of the young officer.

"I cannot consent to go three or four hundred leagues out of my way without it being by force of arms," said Zeb flatly.

"I understand your difficulty," said the governor. "I will give you a certificate showing that you were obliged to make this journey against your will. I would like you to dine with me tonight, and tomorrow you will be taken to a village nearby, where an escort will take you to Chihuahua. It will be led, incidentally, by the lieutenant who headed the force of cavalry we sent recently into the country of the Pawnees on the Arkansas River."

"Just answer one question, Your Excellency," said Zebulon. "Which is the greater infringement of national territory—you sending a party of Spanish horses six hundred miles into American territory, or me, with a small band of soldiers, losing my way in a search for the Red River and mistakenly entering Spanish territory?"

"I don't understand you," said the governor.

"You don't understand me because you don't want to," replied Zeb. On that they parted.

The next day, under escort, Pike set out on a journey through the interior of what was then called New Spain. He was reunited with Dr. Robinson at Albuquerque, New Mexico. The doctor, on arriving at Santa Fe, had discovered that Pike's camp was on the Rio del Norte (Rio Grande) and not on the Red River as Zeb thought. He had considered coming back and warning Zebulon, but decided against it because Zebulon and his party were too weak to move anyway. They had to stay where they were to survive.

Robinson said he had been closely questioned about the expedition, but had been well treated. The two made the jounrey together, under escort, to Chihuahua, where they were questioned by the Commandant General Don Nimesio Salcedo. Here all Pike's papers were scrutinized again, and twenty-one documents removed. Though General Salcedo treated Pike well, he took the position that Pike was a spy. He wrote to General Wilkinson, Pike's commanding officer, saying that Pike had violated Spanish territory on purpose, and the Spanish ambassador in Washington even lodged a protest with President Jefferson.

But President Jefferson had been informed fully of Pike's expedition and replied that Pike's orders were to go up the Arkansas River and return by the Red River. He had mistaken his way, and that was all there was to it. Nonetheless the Spanish, distrustful of America, would not accept this explanation. Finally diplomatic relations between the two countries were broken off. The war with Spain, so long delayed, broke out under President Polk many years later.

Despite General Salcedo's belief that Zebulon was a spy, Pike was sent back to the United States. He did not waste time on the journey, but made secret notes of the strength and disposition of the Spanish forces in New Spain, their arms, the position of forts and rivers—in fact all that would be of use to the United States should war break out with Spain. These notes he hid by stuffing them down the barrels of his men's muskets.

When he got back to the United States, after an extensive journey through the Spanish territory, he had a mass of information which was to prove of great value to the war department later. Even while a semi-prisoner of the Spanish, Zebulon Pike remained a soldier, working for his country.

Meeting with Jefferson

CHAPTER FOURTEEN

ZEBULON PIKE got back to the United States July 1, 1807. It was a year since he had set out up the Arkansas River on his exploration of the western and southern portions of the Louisiana Purchase territory, and he found the country in a turmoil. Aaron Burr, former Vice President, had been arrested on a charge of treason, and to Zebulon's astonishment he found that his own name was beclouded in the charges brought against Burr.

In a nutshell the situation was that Burr was charged with a plot to set up, by force of arms and with Spanish aid, an independent nation west of the Alleghenies in the Louisiana Purchase territory. There was a great deal of evidence to show that he had been in contact with Spanish agents and with many of the settlers in the territory, who thought that their own interests would best be served by breaking away from the United States and declaring themselves an independent nation.

General Wilkinson had warned President Jefferson of this plot. As a consequence, Burr was arrested and tried. The trial opened in Richmond, Virginia, only two months before Zebulon was returned from New Spain by the Spanish. Wilkinson traveled to Richmond to give evidence. But as the trial proceeded, it became clear that Wilkinson himself may well have been involved in the infamous Burr conspiracy. Conversations and letters between the two men were brought out; these cast grave doubts on Wilkinson's own loyalty to the United States. It began to look as though General Wilkinson, although commanding officer of the United States Army at the time, had been so deeply in league with Burr that he had moved troops to certain strategic positions to aid Burr in the proclamation of the new nation.

What then had Zebulon Pike really been doing? the public demanded. Had he indeed been on an exploratory expedition? Or was he an advance agent of Burr and Wilkinson, contacting the Spanish perhaps for help, with secret orders from General Wilkinson to get himself into Spanish territory so he would be "arrested" and thus could communicate with the higher officials of the Spanish government?

Many people pointed out that, whereas the Rogers and Clark expedition to the Pacific had been personally authorized by President Jefferson, Pike's expedition had not had direct Presidential sanction. Rather, it had been ordered by General Wilkinson, who was now strongly suspected of treason.

Returning then from his heroic journey, Zebulon found himself not a national hero but a man under suspicion, coolly treated by his superiors, warily handled by his fellow officers, and the target of scurrilous and anonymous letters in the newspapers of the day.

He was not a man to endure such a situation patiently. He had been given his orders by his commanding officer, and he had carried them out to the best of his ability, in circumstances where many others would have given up. That was his position, and he never wavered from it nor from his loyalty to General Wilkinson, though the case against Wilkinson became blacker as the trial of Burr proceeded.

In the end Burr, after a fair trial, was acquitted of charges of treason, but public opinion ran so strongly against him that he fled to Europe. Wilkinson was then subjected to a series of court martials and investigations. He emerged with no treason proven against him, but it was shown that at times he had received sums of money from the Spanish.

Zebulon was surrounded by malicious whispers and suspicions. Few persons stopped to consider that a young officer, leading a handful of men hobbling on frozen feet, without artillery, with little ammunition and few stores, would hardly have been chosen to set up an independent nation in the western regions of the Louisiana Purchase. Zeb, to clear his name, finally wrote to the Secretary of War, Henry Dearborn, demanding an official statement on his two expeditions.

Dearborn replied, saying that while the expeditions had not been ordered by the President, they had been undertaken on the orders of General Wilkinson with the full knowledge of the War Department, that the President had approved of them, and had reported to the Congress on them in flattering terms, and that his work was deeply appreciated by both the President and the Congress.

"You may rest assured that your services are held in

high estimation by the President of the United States,"
Dearborn wrote, "and if any opinion of my own can afford
you satisfaction, I very frankly declare that I consider the
public much indebted to you for the enterprising, per-
severing and judicious manner in which you have per-
formed them."

That was enough for Zebulon. He had done his duty
as ordered.

But it was not enough for the public. For years he was
spoken of as a dark figure; and even after his death,
lengthy and laborious studies were undertaken to prove
that he had had "secret" orders involving treason to the
United States. He was the victim of a "smear campaign"
which persisted for a hundred years.

There was nothing he could do about it. One man
cannot deal with a thousand rumors. He went back to his
work as a professional soldier, getting his notes together
and finally publishing a full report of his journeys up the
Arkansas, in the Rockies and Sangre de Cristo Mountains,
and then in New Spain.

Meanwhile he had not forgotten the men who had been
left behind. A few months after his own return to the
United States, he was able to report that all his men were
back. He now made every effort he could to obtain double
pay for his men for their extraordinary services to their
country. Double pay had been given the men of the Lewis
and Clark expedition. A committee of inquiry went into
the matter. It was a committee of the House of Repre-
sentatives, and it noted that the whole expedition had had
the approval of the President. The Committee recom-
mended special compensation for the men. So did Secretary of War Dearborn. But the Congress itself refused
to vote the funds.

Men like Dougherty and Sparks, who had become crippled by frostbite during the expedition were given the usual small pension awarded to discharged soldiers. It was enough to eat on but not enough to live on, and Pike became increasingly bitter against the politicians who were niggardly to private soldiers because of their suspicions of generals.

Zeb's wife Clarissa joined him at Natchitoches on his return, but she had sad news for him. Shortly after he left to go up the Arkansas, she had given birth to a son, but the baby had died. Pike's son had been born and buried without his ever having seen the child. It was a terrible blow to Zebulon, for he had wanted a son to follow him as a soldier, as he had followed his father. He had a daughter of whom he was very fond, but a son to keep the name of Pike on the rolls of the United States Army was his greatest desire.

In September, 1807, Pike, his wife Clarissa, and his four-year-old daughter, also named Clarissa, sailed from New Orleans to New York. The population of New York in those days was only 70,000, but it was fast becoming the biggest city in the United States, second only to Philadelphia. Talk of the coming Presidential election filled every drawing room and club. There was talk also of a possible war with England, which was engaged in a life-and-death struggle with Napoleon's France. American ships were being searched by the British Navy on the high seas. American seamen were being pressed into the British service.

From New York Zebulon and his family journeyed to Washington, to find the capital full of politicians and office seekers. Legislation before the Congress provided for the establishment of an expanded army of 32,830 men, including militia.

Zebulon applied to Secretary of War Dearborn for command of a corp in the new army. But the taint of Wilkinson and Burr still clung to him. Dearborn probably would have been glad enough to promote the young captain. But with a Presidential election in the offing and public opinion strongly against Wilkinson, he dared not do so. Instead, he offered Zebulon the rank of a major in a rifle corps. That would mean a return to the western frontier and perhaps some backwoodsman with political pull as his superior officer.

Bitter over public suspicion and neglect of his men, Zebulon thought of resigning. He had been offered command of the New Jersey militia by the governor of that state, and he seriously considered resigning from the regular army and taking up this appointment. But the call of the professional army was too strong.

His father had fought through the Revolutionary War and was still, in his old age, an officer of the United States Army. Zebulon swallowed his pride and accepted promotion to major in the Sixth Infantry, in command of a small detachment at Bellefontaine at the junction of the Arkansas and Mississippi rivers.

He managed to get his younger brother, George Pike, admitted to West Point, and there was a prospect here of the Pike line continuing in the army. Zeb sent a letter of advice to his brother on the conduct of an officer and a gentleman. You must behave, he wrote, as becomes the son of a man who was an old patriot and soldier. You must not seek to make a splash by spending money recklessly. And you must pay close attention to your grammar in writing letters.

Before he left Washington, Pike was presented to President Jefferson at the White House. It was a remarkable meeting between the tall, lean, graceful President of tremendous learning and the slight, weather worn, self-taught officer who had traveled far into the lands that Jefferson had added to the United States.

Zebulon reported later that the President received him with "great attention and respect." They talked of Zebulon's journey into the Rockies and of the huge peak, "like a blue cloud," that he had discovered. They talked of the Pawnees and the Osages and the Sioux and the Utes and the other tribes that Zebulon had met and addressed in the name of the President—their "Great White Father."

Jefferson was especially interested in the plant life of the new region, for he was always interested in horticulture and loved gardening. Zebulon told him of the rolling grasslands of the west, of the huge timber stands, and the uncountable herds of buffalo in the new territory. Perhaps the President for a moment envied this young officer who at the age of twenty-eight had ventured so far into the unknown and was now a major in the United States Army. He invited Zebulon to called on him again, and, at their second interview, Zebulon asked the President's permission, as his commander-in-chief, to publish the journals of his expedition to the headwaters of the Mississippi and into the Rockies.

The permission was granted readily, for the President hoped that the publication of these journals would arouse public interest in the vast territory acquired by the Louisiana Purchase and would lead to settlement of the lands. Zebulon immediately set to work, and, two years later, his journals were published. The printer was John Binns of Philadelphia, who was the first to print the United States Constitution. The publication of Pike's journals had a tremendous effect on the public. Immediately, Pike's name was on everyone's lips. It became a household word, and for a while at least, the whispering campaign against him died down. The journals were printed in London, and then in France, Holland, and Germany. In a short while Zebulon had become an international figure.

Meanwhile, the war talk grew. It seemed that the United States, against its will, was to be plunged into a war with England for which it was totally unprepared.

Eight new regiments were raised by order of the Congress, but they were dispersed about the country, some along the eastern seaboard, some along the Mississippi and the Ohio, and others along the Gulf of Mexico. The men were ill-equipped and ill-trained. The Congress decided that the port of New Orleans would be an obvious target for the enemy if war came. If the port was captured by the British, the commerce of the whole Mississippi valley would be paralyzed.

Pike, with a battalion of the Sixth Infantry Regiment, was rushed to New Orlean as the spearhead of defense. His commanding general was to be Wilkinson, and once again the old hostilities against the two were revived.

Zebulon never wavered in his loyalty to his commanding officer. But it was a loyalty that cost him dearly and made him many enemies. Pike was ordered to establish a cantonment at Terre aux Boeufs, twelve miles south of New Orleans, and labored for weeks in the humid heat, plagued by mosquitoes and a shortage of supplies, to establish a base there.

He had no doctors for the hundreds of men under his command and had to tend to the sick himself. The area swarmed with mosquitoes, and half his men were soon down with malaria. With the remainder, he struggled to drain the land and build levees and put up buildings. His supplies of flour turned moldy in the damp heat. Villainous contractors supplied him with meat crawling with maggots. The site had been chosen by Wilkinson, contrary to his instructions from the War Department, which had advised the use of higher ground north of New Orleans.

But Wilkinson could not resist the prospect of profit. He chose the swampy land of Terre aux Boeufs, paying a rent of $640 to the proprietor, who not only got his rent but had thirty acres of his swampland drained by the army and converted into land suitable for growing sugar cane. Wilkinson, it was suspected, made his own profit on the deal. It must have been obvious to Zebulon that the site was a poor one, but he remained loyal to his commanding officer and, as a result, was attacked by the press. Finally, the site was abandoned on the orders of the War Department, but not until several hundred men had died of malaria.

A congressional investigation was held, but Zebulon was cleared of any blame. All the witnesses testified to his care for his men and the fact that he had personally tried to doctor them when they were ill and no doctors were available.

Wilkinson was ordered to take the greater body of his troops to Forts Adams and Natches to the north, leaving a small garrison in New Orleans. He finally obeyed these orders, leaving Zebulon in charge of the New Orleans garrison. Pike did his work so well that he was appointed lieutenant colonel. But Wilkinson's enemies were now out for Pike's scalp, and he was removed from his New Orleans command and transferred to the Fourth Massachusetts Regiment in Mississippi Territory.

And so the months went by, with Wilkinson's enemies getting at him through the loyal Pike. But Pike's efficiency as an officer, his unswerving insistence on discipline, his ability to make shambling raw recruits into good soldiers in a matter of months, could not be ignored. At a time when high command in the United States Army went to men with political pull and full purses rather than to professional soldiers, Pike, on his reputation alone, was reckoned one of the best junior-grade officers in the army.

Then late in June of 1812 the inevitable occurred. War was declared between the United States and Britain. Two weeks later Pike was promoted to full colonel. Strategy called for an attack on Canada, and Pike wrote to the man to whom he had always been loyal, General Wilkinson.

"If we go into Canada," he said, "you will hear either of my fame or of my death."

CHAPTER FIFTEEN

Death of a Soldier

CHAPTER FIFTEEN

T HE UNITED STATES entered what was to become known as the War of 1812 utterly unprepared. Its standing army numbered only a few thousand professional soldiers, and these were scattered throughout the country, in places as far apart as New Orleans and New York. Colonel Zebulon Pike, thirty-three years of age and one of the most experienced officers in the skeleton army, was given command of a new regiment, the Fifteenth Foot, and was to be attached to the brigade of General Joseph Bloomfield.

The regiment existed only on paper, and Zebulon had first of all the task of raising seven hundred recruits to fill out its rolls. Not only had he to enlist these men, but he had also to train them. And it was all to be done in a great hurry. Zebulon took command of the regiment in June and by the end of July had enlisted seven hundred men who were put under training at Staten Island. Physical standards for recruits were not strict. Size did not matter. Recruits were rejected only if they suffered from ruptures, scurvy or sore legs. Boys from fourteen to eighteen could join if they had a letter of consent from their parents, but they were to be employed only as musicians.

Supplies were almost impossible to get. There was no organized quartermaster corps for the army, and Zebulon had to scrounge around for food and clothing for his men. Muskets were issued, but they were without flints and in desperation Zebulon scoured the New York area for barrels of flints so that his men could have some target practice. Many of them had never fired a gun in their lives. Just as the flints arrived, Zebulon received orders to transport his men up the Hudson to Albany where they would be trained further.

When the men got to Albany, late in August of 1812, they were without tents or supplies. The drill ground was a rough area, only recently cleared of trees. There was time for a little rushed training—sufficient instruction for the men to know how to set the flints, prime the pans, insert the cartridges with a ramrod, and fire their pieces. But they were still nothing but a horde of confused recruits when orders came to go to Plattsburg in upper New York state. All expected that the invasion of Canada was now to take place. But they were disappointed.

Zebulon did, however, lead a small force into the Province of Quebec, but it was a minor thrust to feel out the enemy's strength. He met a force of Canadian militia and Indians, defeated them and burned their camp. But on his way back to Plattsburg, he ran into a company of American troops. Discipline was so bad and nerves so jittery that the two groups of Americans fired on each other, and several men were killed before the mistake was discovered.

It was a terrible start, but it was to be expected for the men of the American Expeditionary Force at Plattsburg were soldiers in name only. They had received no drill, no training in arms. They had no discipline and no sense of pride either in their regiment or their army. And the civilian contractors who supplied the army with food, blankets, and tents saw in the war merely a great opportunity for profit. They sold shoddy goods at outrageous prices and pocketed their profits without a qualm of conscience.

Zebulon found one army contractor, Tench Coxe, cutting blankets in half and selling the two halves as whole blankets. One day one of his sergeants came to Zebulon with such a blanket.

"Look at this, sir," he said. "It is all the men have for covering."

The blanket was so thin that a man could almost see through it, and it measured three feet by four feet. Outraged at this Zebulon folded the blanket up, put it in an envelope, and sent it to Secretary of War Eustis. Eustis had replaced Dearborn, who had now been given an active command. But the protest did no good. Coxe had too many connections in Washington, and he continued as supplier to the shivering soldiers who faced a winter in northern New York state with such wretched equipment.

Zebulon then put his men to work erecting log huts for shelter. He was an old hand at this, but the work went slowly and it was Christmas before he had shelters up for all the men. With the advance of winter, the death toll of the wretched American Army on the Hudson rose daily. By the end of December a hundred men in Zebulon's regiment alone had died of exposure. The higher officers refused to share the hardship of their men. They returned to comfortable homes in New York, leaving their juniors to take over.

Only two colonels remained with the troops at Plattsburg—Zebulon Pike and Cromwell Pearce of the Sixteenth Regiment. When the other senior officers had left their men, what little morale or discipline there was among them evaporated. The soldiers felt that they had been deserted both by their officers and by their country. Shivering by night and by day with inadequate clothing, compelled to eat food that was rotten, they became mutinous and riotous.

Brawls broke out day and night among the men, and several were murdered in drunken fighting. Pike wrote to the Inspector General at Washington, warning that the whole army at Plattsburg was in danger of collapse before even a shot was fired. But there was no cure for the situation. The War Department was inept, if not corrupt, and the whole nation was demoralized, for the war was going very badly. Two American attempts at an invasion of Canada, one from Detroit and the other from the American side of Niagara Falls, had been repulsed. Nobody really believed that the third invasion of Canada, planned as an assault on Montreal, had any hope of succeeding.

Nobody, that is, except Zebulon Pike and his fellow officer, Colonel Cromwell Pearce. These two, remaining with their men, attempted by example to build up the morale of the men and drill them into discipline. After a while the strain was too much for Zebulon. He had never been physically strong, despite the many hardships he endured, and late in December of 1812, because of a raging fever, he had to quit camp for a short while.

He was back soon, however, and with a revolutionary plan. The army was still drilling according to the Manual of Arms laid down by Von Steuben in the Revolutionary

War. Zebulon decided to drill his regiment in the French method—a method which had made such excellent soldiers of the French infantry under Napoleon. The other officers laughed at him, but finally the Fifteenth Foot under Colonel Pike was acknowledged the best regiment in the expeditionary force.

Zebulon got his reward for all this work in the spring of 1813. By that time what remained of the dwindling American Army around Plattsburg had been welded into a disciplined body. Now came orders to march overland to Sackett's Harbor on the east end of Lake Ontario. Pike went first with the Fifteenth Regiment.

There was still three feet of snow on the ground and one of his men froze to death on the march. Many others had their feet so badly frostbitten that they had to be amputated. But shortly after his arrival at Sackett's Harbor, he got news of his promotion to brigadier general. General Dearborn, pleading illness, was absent from his command. The invasion of Canada, then, when it came, would be in the hands of Brigadier General Zebulon Pike.

Plans were now altered. Montreal was not to be attacked, but rather the city of York (the present-day Toronto) at the western end of Lake Ontario. The Americans would be taken down the lake in ships and assault York from landing barges. The responsibility of the assault rested squarely with Zebulon, and he was overjoyed at the prospect.

He had under his command four thousand troops including his own highly trained Fifteenth Regiment. He believed he would succeed. Before the troops embarked on the transports, orders concerning their conduct, issued by their general, Zebulon Pike, were read to them. Private property was to be respected. Plundering was forbidden under pain of death. Any of the enemy who surrendered were to be protected. Before setting out, Zebulon wrote his aging father: "If success attend my steps, honor and glory await my name—if defeat, still shall it be said we died like brave men; conferred honor even in death on the American name."

The squadron sailed on April twenty-third, but was forced to anchor off York for three days because of a storm. The men fretted, visualizing the building up of their enemy's defenses. Zebulon alone remained calm. Every detail had been worked out. There were plenty of barges to take the men ashore to establish a beachhead. Zeb had been over and over his invasion plans with his officers, and each unit knew precisely what it was to do. There were ample supplies, and discipline was good.

At dawn on the morning of April 27, the storm had blown itself out and the guns of the invasion fleet spoke. The thunder of the cannon rumbled over the flat waters of the lake, and after the first few salvos lanterns were hauled to the masts of the invasion fleet, signaling "Boats away."

The men were already in the boats, waiting in the gray dawn alongside the transports. Zebulon was in a barge that contained some of the men of his own Fifteenth Regiment. They cheered him as he stepped into the barge, and the word went over from boat to boat "Pike's coming with us." As a general officer he could have remained on board the warship *Madison,* which was the flagship of the invasion fleet. But Zebulon preferred to go with his men and share with them the terrible slaughter of gaining a beachhead.

The shore batteries now opened up, firing at the barges as they came slowly through the water, rowed by sailors from the fleet. Several were hit, but most got through the enemy cannonade. Pike was among the first to land.

The small beach at the edge of the lake was swept by rifle fire.

"Clean out those riflemen," Zebulon ordered, and his Fifteenth Regiment swept forward toward the enemy works. Many of the defenders were Indians. Seeing the Americans sweeping down on them in large numbers, they started to run, shouting, "Too much Yankee! Too much Yankee!"

The rifle pits of the British were soon occupied, and still the Americans pressed forward toward the shore batteries. Some of these they took after sharp little bayonet fights. Some fell without a struggle. The ships offshore were now concentrating their fire on the main fort guarding the town. Pike urged his men forward to within four hundred yards of this fort, and then sent back for artillery with which to silence it. Suddenly a white flag was raised on the fort.

"Go forward and see whether the British commander is prepared to formally surrender the town," Pike ordered one of his aides. As he spoke, a musket was fired and a young officer near Pike fell to the ground, badly wounded. Pike looked around. Smoke and dust obscured his view, and he found himself almost alone with the young officer. In a surge of pity he forgot for a moment his position as commanding general. He picked the officer up and carried him back to the water's edge, where he handed him over to some of the new arrivals. Then he returned to the area before the fort and rejoined his staff. Colonel Pearce was nearby, and Zebulon asked him whether there was any formal news of the British surrender. Pearce shook his head.

A soldier appeared out of the dust and battlesmoke. "We've got a British prisoner for questioning, sir," he said.

A second later there was a tremendous explosion. A

British magazine, only a few yards away, had blown up. Rocks and debris whistled through the air, and when the dust had settled, Pike was lying on his face, his back a pulped and bleeding mass. A huge rock had gone clear through his body. Colonel Pearce ran to him, and Pike said, "I'm done for, Pearce. Keep up the attack. You must take command now."

He was rushed to the water's edge on a stretcher and taken aboard the warship *Madison*. The naval surgeon who examined him shook his head. The wound was mortal, and there was nothing he could do.

From far ashore there came burst after burst of cheering. York had fallen—the first important American victory of the war. Pike smiled at the thought, and, with the smile still on his face, he died. He was thirty-four years of age.

Pike's body was taken back to Sackett's Harbor and buried in a cemetery outside Fort Tompkins. The grave was marked only by a wooden slab. Six years later the body was moved to a new cemetery near Madison Barracks which had just been completed, and a larger wooden marker was set up over it. But the grave was neglected, the marker rotted away, and within a few years no one could say for sure where Brigadier General Zebulon Montgomery Pike was buried. What are presumed to be his remains now rest in a grave marked with a small granite headstone half a mile east of Sackett's Harbor.

When news of the taking of York and the death of General Pike was reported, Zebulon's name was on every tongue. Overnight he became a national hero. President Madison paid a special tribute to him in an address to Congress, and flags were flown at half-mast. Tributes were paid to him by the leading men of the nation. A warship, built at Sackett's Harbor, was christened the *General Pike* in his honor, and engravers struck off thousands of portraits of the young general. These were eagerly bought and displayed in homes from Boston to New Orleans. Plaques and monuments to his memory were erected in several states. Congress voted a pension for his widow. The men of his regiment agreed that the regimental standard should be dressed in mourning each year on the anniversary of his death.

But Zebulon Montgomery Pike had himself, in his lifetime, unwittingly picked his own monument—the great, grim peak on the front range of the rockies in Colorado which became known as Pike's Peak. He had seen it first as a "small blue cloud" on the horizon. He had struggled for days to get to its base. He had striven, shivering in cotton clothing and up to his waist in snow, to climb it and had had to turn back. But, as the years went by, the mountain became his and his alone. The marker on his grave rotted; the mountain stood. His grave was lost; the mountain remained—a monument to the strength in the man which had itself been like the mountain: rugged, courageous, enduring, and faithful.

Mountains have been officially named for many illustrious men. But Pike's Peak was named for him by the common consent of the people of America, in whose service he had toiled as a soldier to explore the farthest reaches of their country, and in whose defense he had lost his life on the field of battle at the age of thirty-four.